Be Wise At All Times.

Muckraker's Folly

A Gasp From Talking Points Factory

by

Allen M. D. Muckraker

Muckraker's Folly

Allen M. D. Muckraker

ISBN-13: 978-1479332984
ISBN-10: 1479332984
Printed in the United States of America

First Printing

About The Author

Mr. Allen M. D. Muckraker is a master of many trades. He is an accomplish graduate of a Bachelors Degree in Business Management and eagerly pursuing a Masters Degree in the same discipline. As a writer, he has published two novels, a memoir and multiple eBooks. Dedicated to the art of writing and revealing constructive information to the masses, Mr. Muckraker is honored to share his suggestions and experience with his countrymen. You should expect the unexpected, as in sudden impact. If you have high-blood-pressure do not read this book.

Author: Allen M. D. Muckraker ©

Allen M. D. Muckraker

About The Book

This read is mitigated on high adrenaline. The author emulates real life issues that are repugnant at best. If you are not grounded in the positive you could find yourself in the same predicament as the crazies. If you are one of the infidels who can not take a serious joke go read something else. You do not belong. Now if you pledge not to burn down your house or hurt yourself with hot chocolate coffee, I promise to keep you entertained for laughs: end on end. Certain parts of this book: not suited for under age kids. You are the parent; figure it out. I hope you don't expect me to say what goes on in your house. Good, now that I've gotten rid of all of the fainted hearts, let's move on.

Author: Allen M. D. Muckraker ©

Muckraker's Folly

Acknowledgements

To a special person who contributed
more than was expected:

Mrs. Muckraker

Extended gratitude I also imparts to
the children who chose me:

The Junior Muckrakers

Muckraker's Folly

A Gasp From Talking Points Factory

Where Else?

Allen M. D. Muckraker

Muckraker's Folly

Table of Contents

Where Else?

Open Minded

Where else but in a Vladimir Putin Russia could there be found Pussy Riot with lots of Russian fans supporting it. Thus, Virginia's young men wishes that they were sentence to two years in labor camp with the three fresh meats. The European Union and the United States condemned Russia for such an outrageous ruling on the lewd vaginal bunch: as unbalanced. How be it, we also have our own pussy riot right here in the U.S.A as Mama Cougars goes on the prowl in our schools.

No harsh sentencings have ever or will ever deter or tame the heated crotch. If my son comes home and announces that Ms. Tulip, his teacher had done him in, I would reply, well done my son. You have succeeded where your dad has miserably failed. Where were all of these horny unclad teachers when I was growing up? The best I got from my teach was a hit up the head and a rough send off to my grandmother for a Groundhog Day of more scolding. So, you are mad at me for saying that. The way I see it is that it is better for Ms. Tulip to have sex with my son than with her dog. It's quite obvious and factual from the information I've gathered that many women are now being screwed by their big dogs. This of-course is mostly a white thing. Black people don't like hairy uncommonly or unsanitary Evolution-ners as sex partners. They don't believe in fang clawed evolution-ners getting too close to the pecker or vagina.

Mrs. Muckraker told me that one of her friend's husband have the dog sleeping in the bed with him, and when the wife goes close to her husband: the dog growls. It won't be long before there's a new niche of governmental protected group. Money talks and bullshit walks. Congress has no morals. Some of our Senators and Representatives will vote for anything that has the smell of corporate moneys attune to it.

On the other hand, if my daughter proclaimed that Mr. Jones had his way with her, and that she is no longer a virgin, I would charge my shotgun and shoot the bastard. Yes, that's right; there seems to be some bias in me. My, daughters must be undefiled until marriage, no whoring around as the likes of the masses. If you disagree, keep your distance, and by the way, make it a rule to stay on the opposite end of my trigger finger.

In conclusion, the moral of the story is that whether you are on a Pussy Riot in Russia, or a horny cherry Cougar hunting in U.S. schools, it just seems like all licentious pussy goes to jail. Protect your meow from unlawful behavior.

Warning! Do not go any further. This book was designed to corrupt you, but if you like it buy copies for your friends. You can read this entire book free if you are an Amazon kindle member.

Where else but in the United States of America can you find exceptional patriotism/a patriotic citizen? Let's take a crack at it. Patriotism: "A citizen's devotion and national pride to his or her country. Another way to look at it if you are an American Republican, Democrat, Independent, Green Party and others: A Spirited citizen who is civically/community minded, nationalistic, loyal, irredentist, uninformed true-blue, chauvinistic and an uneducated/educated personality who votes in contras to his or her wellbeing, such as when a welfare recipient votes for a political candidate who vows to abolish the nanny welfare state. This book is design to make you mad, laugh out loud or get a life. You should expect the unexpected.

Sudden impact was what we agreed on; too late to stop it now. However, there are other stories in this book that are more tempered; on the other hand, if you are a closet person who is actually vulgar in nature only in your house, you have been caught. There's always someone watching.

Where else but in the United States Of America could a hard working, bootstraps-hanging red blooded American citizen get a feeling that the tide of the nation is as such: citizens be dammed. Decades ago there was an American ingenuity, and it built a car with a small three cylinder engine that turns an electric generator that powered the little automobile. The poor Americans loved it, because the miles per gallon (MPG) was outrageous. Due to the doings of our crooked government, every single one of those economical marvels were bought back from their owners at no less-than $30,000.00 plus and sent to the desert of Arizona to be crushed into little bits and pieces. The 99% have no representatives in our government. The Congress and Supreme Court serves the Corporate State.

Where else but in The United States Of America can a profitable cooperation such as Boeing Aircraft pays its CEO (Company Executive Officer) eighteen million dollars plus and pays little or no taxes. Abbott and Motorola also pay their CEO's more than they pay in taxes. By the way, this should not be a riddle, in view of the fact that if you haven't notice, the prevailing trend is that CEO's are not responsible for anything that goes wrong in their companies. Their sole purpose is to get paid, assure that dividends are minuscule, have their way with those that are trying to circumvent the glass-ceiling, and financially enforce political speech for a person. The Supreme Court say that they can do that: show the financial ass of their company's personhood.

Where else, but In Saudi Arabia could a woman be awarded 200 lashes for being gang raped, and the government defends the punishment? But hold the phone, because she could have gotten the nuclear option: death by stoning. A few years pass I was in Iraq on a contracting gig, and had the dishonorable opportunity to interview 7 tribal chiefs on the same subject of sex, be it casual or not. If the woman is not married to the man who's penis has entered into her vagina. The default evil goes to the woman, and since the woman is now defiled/besmirched an honor killing must occur.

Oh! So I hear you say, they are so backwards over there. Well, listen to this. Let me bring you into our Christian dogma/canon (Law) which had the same or similar recompense for whoring around. If Jesus did not challenge the self righteous Judeal stoning bunch to throw the first stone if they themselves were without faults, we Christians would be also stoning infidels today, and rightfully doing so. Many in our nation need a stoning sentence.

Where else, but in The United States Of America, the pinnacle of human rights, and womanlike's, would a presidential candidate declare a deviant war on women by unveiling his Big Binder of Women and a Mascot List of affluent and grassroots pussycats. Ah! Where else?

Where else, but in The United States Of America, in a Union of social justice would the obvious be ignored by millennial sleazes, that the Boy Scouts organization have been an incubator for bottom-hole sex? Muckraker now recommends that Moms send their boys to the Girls Scouts. At-least a licentious act would proclaim his manhood. Ah ha! Where else?

Where else, but within The United States Of America, the manufacturing genesis of fairness, would a Republic-Party-conned-man or a Republic-Party-conned-woman be proven absolutely correct in all their efforts to stamp out voter fraud. The Democratic Party should be in a frenzy of joy right now, since the most recent egregious law indictment of voter fraud in the year 2012 have been the operatives of the Republic-canned-Party. Muckraker now recommends that the law initiate a search in an effort to find 78000 live kicking dead people on the GOP's voters roll. And not only that, every garbage-can behind a Republic-conned-Party registration drive boot should be check for Democratic registration forms.

Opportunity

Where else but in the United States Of America can anyone in the world aspire to greatness? Where Else? However, in these millennial times Americans are not aspiring to greatness. They are smoking dope and taking advice from Talking-Heads who gets paid for making chaos: The better the bedlam; the higher the ratings; the more highly paid the Talking-Heads. We have been overwhelmed by our ridiculous folly as the foreigners take over Silicon Valley.

Where else but in The United States Of America can a poor dunce complete high school, get an airplane license at age 22, complete a four year degree and a few courses less his Masters degree? Where Else?

Where else but in These United States Of America could smarter people than teachers find a specialty job to take aspiring teacher's certification test? Due to this enlightenment of the new brand of honesty in our educated community, Muckraker is now @ liberty to ask a question. *Were these teachers fired-up GOP risk takers—or—Dems* on the verge of conversion? Man it's hard to make-up stories like this. Do not correct my English grammar.

Politics

On August 26, 2012 a talking head was frustrated in as much as to say that Hurricane Isaac was oppressing the Republican Party convention in Tamper, Florida. The Republicans seams to have a curse of the hurricanes: McCain and Gustaf, Katharina and Bush now the Mormon's god and Isaac. Furthermore, what else can anyone expect from a malevolent amalgamation. The Political party is an entity for evil accomplishments. The elite political well heeled club members stole from the poor and give it to the rich. For a period of ten years or more moneys that should have been going into the peoples treasury was not collected on the account that those who did not pay the taxes would provide for the poor. The trickledown effect never occurred as many more poor Americans were given pink-slips as choice to collect food-stamps.

During a catastrophic hurricane named Katharina, a prominent Republican Lady tells its party members who were at that time wearing funny hats at their convention how to become Americans. She explained, "let us take off our Republican hats, and put on our American hats." I knew it all along, but now I've got proof that scoundrels are resident aliens.

In this light, let's take a deeper look on how they brought the hurricane seasonal curse on themselves. One of the 2012 initial Republican Party's candidate's choice for president was Newt Gingrich, once Speaker of congress. He is a good example of how to treat your spouse. The model espoused particularly emphasizes thee action to take if she's dying of cancer: promptly get rid of her during her greatest time of need, and marry another immediately. The physiological sensation from the head of the penis may have been more important than the fortitude to comfort a dying spouse. So, from inception, he was a walking omen due to Christian biblical rules. He's presently living in adultery. His first wife is not dead and he has remarried another. This is a rebellion against Christian rules and values. Not only that, according to an interview given on one of the agents of immoral TV by his first and true wife, the Newt wanted acceptance from her to whore around, per se. We really don't care if the information is true or not. The basic tenet of righteousness implies avoidance of such malevolent vessels. Nevertheless my brothers embraced him as repentant even-though his sins were as bright as the sun.

Added to its evils, the party's next eminent pick was Herman Kane. He was definitely a blight to the Right, in view of the fact, that he likes to put his hands on women's legs, especially during job interviews. If you give him a little bit, you'll be working. He even had an occasion where one of his sexual harassment complaints was settled and he didn't even know anything about it. His last gasp before his sudden political death was his introduction of his 999 plan. Any dummy could have seen through this ungodly act due to the fact that if you turned the plan name upside-down there appear to be three sixes (666). This is the mark of the coming beast. Well, no American, not even Republicans would ever accept that number on their tax forms.

And finally, my brothers on the so-called Religious Right have defamed god by supporting a presidential candidate who's beliefs are contrary to our faith. He aspires to become a god someday. This is according to one of his holy books. This belief is in conflict with serving the one true God. My Christian relatives are spineless hypocrites who believe that politics is separated from Christian ethics. For example: the notion is that since God don't know anything about politics, all of the following are justified:

adultery, shooting/murdering people, hatred, slavery, bottom-hole-sex (Log Cabin Republicans)....

On the notion of slavery, remember that Iowa onetime caucus winner: Michel who justified the

(A caucus is a political party meeting usually to select delegates or candidates for up-coming election.)

Southern slave states for their oneness in the brutal act of slavery, and for fighting to keep blacks in chains? Now, hold your breath, if slavery was so justified in righteousness, how come God delivered his people, Israel from the bondage of the Egyptians? They should have been liking it, and not advocating deliverance. Not only that they were delivered, he had them steal all the Egyptians gold as they were leaving a glorious oneness of brutality.

One American minister in the U.S.A explained that the act of taking the Egyptian gold was repayment for the people's suffering due to the fact that they were enslaved. So, what about some compensation for the wrong of American slavery of Black-People? Yap, I said it; reparations for black Americans, given that the Israelis already got theirs? The American coloreds did not get their promised acres of lands and their mules. Ha ha-ha! Muckraker can see all the white people in the Southern States going crazy if this should come to pass.

Want to here more? Mormons say Jesus will have a New Jerusalem in Missouri, U.S.A and another in Israel. That was why Romney say that the capital of Israel is Jerusalem. And if you want to bend the biblical rules a little bit from the marriage tenets of one man, one woman, then all Christians should practice Polygamy. Ah ha, just a few more pussy cats for a pilgrim's journey. None of this is in the bible. What Else?

Where else but in The United States Of America could a vice-president openly shoot a fellow hunter and gets away with it? With that successfully in the bag, he astutely guided the killing of more than 100,000 Iraqis' on the premise of bad intelligence.

Where else but in The United States Of America could rich people co-opt the art of blending in? Governor Mitt Romney: corporations are peoples my friend. On that note, we as citizens should ask questions. When will these people release their birth papers, college transcripts, 10 previous years of Tax statements and the gross of their Cayman Island's bank accounts? Do these people pay taxes? Governor Mitt Romney paraphrased: 47% of Americans are in love with the Federal-Government; they pay no taxes and will not vote for me. Muckraker would like to make it known to the American public that the following people don't pay any taxes: Motorola-Rumsey, Bank Of America Romney, George Romney, Vernon Romney, Romney Marsh, hedge-fund manager Rumsey, Marion Romney, Verizon Communications republican, General Electric Democrats, Boeing Republican. Ok, here are some real ones: NextEra Energy and Pacific Gas & Electric. Who Else? Some of these are dead personhood, but GOP operatives announced that democrats can get them to vote. This is why during the month of September 2012, 75000 live kicking people in Texas were pronounced dead by the GOP. Everything went well until many of these dead people got their dead notices and read them. Thus, they informed the federal government of the scandalous GOP's ruse of removing them from the voting roll.

Where else, but In the not so Great Briton and her daughter our United States Of America could free men achieved worldwide success and would have nothing to do with it? Thus, due to the riotous nature of their western views, and rise to prominence, Middle-East fatwa's were issued. Salman Rushdie capitulated for his book Satanic Verses and signed an erroneous statement asserting his belief in Islam. He now explains that he regretted it. The California film-maker, who set the Middle East in a riotous uproar from Libya to Australia by dishonoring their religious faith, went into hiding. The Taliban welcomes the $100,000 bounty that was placed for his head. The French who have always been on the loosing side of humanity felt left-out; thus, they have published provocative comics of the prophet Mohamed.

But as we Christians rejoice in our self-righteousness towards the conundrum of the Muslims' upheaval in the Middle East and beyond. How be it, in less-than a 24 hour lull of riotous religious activities, Christians were on the defensive. Real Satanic verses had now determined through prominence omen prophets that Jesus had a wife. Lesson learned; the devil has no religious friends.

Muckraker's Folly

Where else but in The United States Of America, it has been recorded, that one of our black president and our first-lady are now farming less than ten acres without a mule on tax payers property at the Whitehouse. And that's not all of it. His Excellency is more than culpable, due to the fact that he has cause an increase in the homemade brewing business in the beautiful state of Colorado. All of this qualitative drinking has been cause by reason that his Excellency is now brewing beer in Abraham Lincoln's dungeon beneath our Whitehouse. Well, there's one opposition member on his side: a drunken republican skinny dipping in the Promised Land. You do not have to believe it. You just have to read it. Ha, haa.....

Where else but in The United States Of America that citizens are duped by the political term energy independence/self-sufficient? The politicians have been using it for decades now, and we Americans are too dumb to figure out the game of idiocy. Muckraker will now tell fellow citizens what must be done to relinquish our dependency on foreign oil. The solution is that we stop buying it. The only countries we should buy oil from should be Mexico and Canada. Aha! I now hear the crazies choking on their saliva. This is a stupid suggestion, they grunt, and I reply you are correct. But, there is one little catch to this solution.

Resolution # 1: the politicians will not be able to fool us any more.

Resolution # 2: The term "drill baby drill" will now be relevant as it becomes a must. The ultimate satisfaction will then be achieved. Would it be gratuitous that we be ungrateful and remove our underpants and bend over and tell the Kings of the Middle East such as Saudi Arabia and Kuwait to kiss our un-royal black and white America a... please complete the previous sentence. And if the British Crown is unable to prevent British Petroleum (BP) from destroying our fisheries in the Gulf Of Mexico, we may just have to bend over pull-down our under-pants for her Majesty also. Heed our warning, and we will save you a reoccurrence of the Boston Tea Party. This time we'll bring back the tea in now the not so Great Britain.

Where else but in The United States Of America that a political pundit name Ryan who benefits from a law he metered through for big oil, so that his family can collect $30,000 each year. As he benefits from government dealings he tells senior citizen that the elderly that comes after them will not have Medicare as they know it for their medical safety-net. Many of these deprived old people are energized by such insincerity coming from the mouth of a rich-man who's a voter of evil political deals that support giant medical companies' research programs. The prices for medication from such fortune five hundred corporations are always set out of the reach of aged Americans. Only in America you can find fools that are synergized by their emotions as they experience the weight of their doing sooner than later.

Where else but in The United States Of America that political party members are motivated to shoot and murder people. It is said that those are the crazy ones. Are there any sane republicans? Colorado Theater Shooter James Holmes is a registered republican. Arizona shooter Jared L. Loughner who shoots Congresswoman Gabrielle Giffords is a registered republican. Wisconsin Sikh Temple shooter Wade Michael Page is a registered republican. Have you gotten the picture? Never get into an enclosed space with republicans. When possible, it may be a potential victims only chance to shoot first and ask questions later when dealing with perturb feints.

Where else but in The United States Of America would the citizens be given a choice of closing federal postal offices. Thus, they will be left in rural areas without adequate mailing services, instead of cutting expenditures on contriving unnecessary wars, giving grants to billionaire oil companies and financing big corporate researches for medicine that the average American Citizen is unable to pay for.

Where else but in The United States Of America does it take a vice-president of the nation to explain that the Grand Old Party would like to put African Americans back in chains. Take care how you understand the politics of the parties that was altered over the years, since the democrats were the culprits holding the chains. A caveat to complement the GOP's conundrum; is that the modern Grand Old Party worshipers, desires not only to get coloreds back in chains, but they also fancy the idea that white poor women should also be shackled to menial existence and in addition endure the recompense of what is coined or misspoken as legitimate-rape.

The GOP's prevailing view of women was solidified by the affluent Grand Old Party's Missourian prince: Todd Akin, as he politicized a woman's right to choose. This conservative Akin is in an identical elitist frame of mind as a French International Bank Monetary Fund minister who purportedly, but forcefully and accurately come-into (ejaculated into) the mouth of the hotel cleaning lady, and after he was content with the act of viciously using a limp French penis as a weapon, he garnered political wit, and discredited her. Then and again if she did not like it, why didn't she bite him on his dick.

By default, the self-serving Todd who has voted 7 times to give himself a governmental financial wage increase has placed all American women in danger as he motivates the rapist to justify an abhorring act. For his political pleasure, it would be acceptable if we return to barbarism and stone our girls at times when they are raped through no fault of their own. All rapes are forceful acts. Statutory rape is a forceful act. The rapist force his or her will on another to have sexual relations with that person who has not reached the legal age of consent. Date rape is a cowardly forceful act: The rapist forces his or her will on another to have sexual relations with a person during or after a date. Muckraker will now reveal his premonition of the GOP's Gang-Num-Star eighteenth century bayonet slinging rape riddle: legitimate rape, forcible rape, and according to a politically aloof Murdock, god intended rape. If there is going to be rape for breakfast Muckraker will definitely start wearing cast iron draws.

By the way, all rapes are bad and when society is absolutely certain that a person has committed the act of rape, that person should be shot one hour after sentencing. Others who motivates their fellow countrymen by folly or political satire (wit, irony, sarcasm, ridicule, and other vices) to indulge in the act of raping others, should be stripped naked in public and upon his or her genitals, there attached with safety pins, 7 ounce of leaded balls. Those who rape children should die by execution as they are being made to jump from the San Francisco Bridge. All those who are against capital punishment present yourself to be dishonored as you voluntarily bends-over and experience the recompense of what you are mistakably defending. There were no cries of murder by the legitimate abortion protesters as we murdered the Iraqis by the thousands due to what was coined: bad intelligence. Therefore, why shouldn't rape victims kill their own? That should get you hypocrites on fire: you charlatans fall to your knees and repent while you have time!

Where else but in The United States of America could two black presidents admit that they were druggies? I love their honesty; one inhale and the other one ate all of the smoke. Where Else? You've got to love it.

Where else but in The United States Of America does the highest court in the land/nation proclaims clear instructions on how to buy your own Senator, congressman/woman and or president. Consequentially, it decrees that you are Citizens United. Where Else?

Where else but in The United States Of America could there be a bad situation concerning gross negligence of oil spilled that halted almost all fishing in the gulf of Mexico. As a consequence of its amplified shortcomings a corporation agreed to be shaken-down by a sitting president? Then, the government turns over all of the money garnered from the loot to a lawyer who then tries to pay the potential plaintiffs as little money as possible to save the scandalous corporation some money, so that the lawyers take of the Chief Executive Officer's (of the United States) loot for the people may be bigger. So much for helping our only Robin Hood of the century... Where Else?

Where else but in The United States Of America in the home of the brave and the land of patriotic Act would citizens be disallowed to vote by their government: Florida, Texas, Kansas, Mississippi, Georgia North Carolina, Pennsylvania, Tennessee. However, we Americans have inundated the world with a façade of being good stewards of voters' rights. Where Else?

Where else but in The United States Of America can a citizen become an elite patriot or jingoistic party member, so proclaimed: a great American. This book was written to make you democrats and republicans mad. Both party members need to get a life.

Join the conservative Movement, since you can easily hide amongst these good people.

Have an explosive incarnated session with a perceived self acclaimed half blind minister:

Muckraker's Folly

Glen. Upon completion, you will be open to receive your fiends, and perhaps your commission.

Defend all bigots vehemently especially if they discharge saliva on senators, and support the current bank financing boycott of all small businesses, in view of the fact that such efforts will help the middle class.

Support tax cuts for the rich, since you play the state lottery, and hope to win big.

Make a bigot sign. To plus that up, get yourself a website.

Go to a Tea Party rally, since you are grounded at home and are vested in retirement, unemployment, secretly acquiring food stamps or collecting social security, thus having nothing else to do with your time.

Show your sign, but hide it when you see a reporter and his or her camera.

Call the talking-heads radio show, then make an outrageous statement about a sitting American president, the repealing of the 14th amendment and give your ultimate allegiance to the doctor who uses the N word on national radio.

Receive your favorite talking-head's blessing that you are a great American. He/she works for your god's networks' and with his blessings the mischievous sprite to block good legislations, disrupt good order and trash hard working loyal Americans will now be your guide. You are now great, patriotic, a stanch cultist/loyalist and do not have to really do any thing realistic to demonstrate your loyalty and love for your country.

Now that you have been blessed, call the other likeminded talking-heads show and increase their ratings. This step is compulsory, since the network is a subcomponent of the wealthy elites.

Do not make the mistake of checking to be sure that talking points are correct. This is none of your concern.

Reiterate a parallel statement as your likeminded talking-heads did, expounding that the other party members are F-ing idiots.

Attend at least one more prominent gathering to tryout your narrow-mindedness. If the former governor of Alaska is schedule to speak, and a $500 fine is levied in order for you to capture a seat, make the sacrifice by using your unemployment benefits;

furthermore, have your family eat less by indulging in illegal activities such as selling your government issued food-stamps. Your objective is a commendable cause, and your wife and kids need to understand that they ought to lend a helping hand in feeding the elitist spirits also, because you hope to be rich some time in the future.

Congratulations you are almost there. You've now made it to the first pinnacle of voting against your own interest. Please repeat these words. "I am an unintelligent person. Say it again. I am an unintelligent person!" Yes!

Now, you do not have to bother with the real task of actually serving your country, since patriotism of the mouth hole is all you need.

In view of the fact, that you have been made a great American, falsely accusing or shooting others is now in play. Place an edited excerpt of a film on your website that does not reveal the entire truth about what a prominent civil rights person wants to convey. This, of course, will wreck the life of that individual, and perhaps anyone else who opposes your ideology. Send a copy of your edited dogma to the American Saudi Arabian prince television networks given that they usually do a perfect job of inflaming imprudent citizens by using this type of material to get the ratings. If you are successful, the government will fire the accused immediately. His majesties American Arabian television networks (FOX News) is quite generous, given that it is allowed to meddle in the internal affairs of the United States. Furthermore, the Republican Party has endorsed the ranting agent, and as a result has been endowed with a one million dollar bribe from his majesties propaganda wing (The FOX News parent company). They will come to your defense; you can do no wrong.

You are now serving your country by using your best judgment, and if you get sued perhaps they will run to your rescue, in view of the facts that they may be bigots to. You have graduated. You are a patriotic, jingoistic conservative, or for better words: a great American. Everywhere you go, your guiding spirit will now lead you in the path of lying, deceitfulness, blindness to all truth and the courage to vote against your own interest.

For actual experience on doing something for your country, and becoming a true patriotic American please start with serving your country first. Oh! Talking points stooges don't have the guts or balls to do that.

Where else but in The United States Of America can a new citizen be aborted by placing them in a room immediately after birth, so that they can die quietly. Many Americans see this as the right of a woman to choose life or death concerning the newborn. It get's even better. Now, in pastimes, it was possible for a citizen to opted in to kill their child if they wanted a girl and the x-ray machine exposed that a boy child was on its way. Once you start the murdering, exceptions will be made for what seems to be extenuating circumstances. One party despises abortion; however, they are on record of giving a religious nod of acceptance where and when democracy is to be expanded. The notion here is that children should not be aborted; however, adults are better murdered to further a country's ideology. Where Else? Ah?

Government Spending

Where else but in The Commonwealth State Of Kentucky in The United States Of America would a private company that was contracted to process State's Medicare claims, and that company denied a poor old sickly American soul of around or about a $1200.00 claim. However, thereafter, the executives had more or less $500 limousine tabs as they gallivant in merriness on the Las Vegas strip with Medicare monies. Where else?

Where else but in The State Of Pennsylvania in The United States Of America that a Mayor name Reed finds financial solace for his beloved city in a trash incinerator. Not even the Fed's could top his genius, given that, he had figured out the Harrisburg cash-cow since 1969. On the other hand, if it was not brilliance, then, it was a case of sleazing the public by paying for a sport's stadium and other come-a-longs by refinancing the cities garbage disposal unit. But if the lawyers had no will in Harrisburg, Pennsylvania, they did find a way for a fee of more than $100,000 each time the cash cow that inhabits the trash incinerator moos. Mayor Reed   milked that cash-cow so habitually that it generated a pending funeral for the city of Harrisburg, to an increase from $12.5 million to $200,000,000. However, no one in the city of Harrisburg knew that it was a covert operation. Thus, the financial overseer of the cities business came upon some divine encouragement to check the records, and as a result found the city of Harrisburg entangled in a $200,000,000 incinerator's deficit as at the same time Mayor Reed was asking for more money. Thus he spilled the beans and all hell broke loose.

Where else but in The oil bless State Of Louisiana in The United States Of America would citizens feel the rising pressure of their elected or appointed masters. The question is, follow our lead? The law in Pennsylvania imprisoned juveniles for a million dollars or more in kickbacks, and made a bank out of a garbage furnace. In the state of Illinois, the chosen administrator of the peoples' business in that state was found on the wrong side of the law, on the question of selling United States congressionally vacated senate seat. He's now an emissary in face down spaces within the presence of his new friend: Bubba. A North or South Dakota lieutenant Governor found his cash cow by kidnapping Native American children for a fee; paid by the government. The State Of Louisiana felt a sense of being left-out; therefore, to be grandfathered in the cogent reason of sleazy government or law enforcement, those in the quandary have devised an incentive to police officers of receiving $15 for each traffic tickets written. How do the citizens of this Grand old Party state get in on the deal? So, if the muckraker was an Officer on the beat in this county, and by writing just 50 traffic tickets each day: $750. Now, I would like to work this system for just five days each week: $3750. Bear in mind that this is just my extra cash. I say, where do I sign up?

But you have not heard the best of reverse government spending yet. You see, Shirley live in the Atlanta area of the American Georgian state. I had to make it plain which Georgia this scoundrel live in. I do not want anyone heading to the beautiful state of Alaska, and looking through their window trying to see the Georgia that is close to Russia and Turkey. With that cleared-up, let's continue...... In Shirley's imagination, as a recollection, she saw the Speaker of the house of congress as he pass out checks (His ill-gotten gains) on the house floor with ease and poise. I do believe that this was a motivating factor in the game of folly. Therefore, she devised no plan, and decided to confront the GOP's peepee (money making machine) without shame and moral prudence. Embolden by her protégé, she tackled the get rich scheme without any fear, and took a $30,000 fee for a vote she cast. Seeing that all representatives sells their votes in one form or another, it was jealousy that done her in, in view of the fact, that she was benefitting directly from her political office, and a three year sentence was levied. Muckraker, suggest that the law forgive this villain, given that she had guts and fortitude to express openly the real deal that has been a plague to the citizens of Georgia for sometime now.

Ok! Muckraker believes that the entire human system is corrupt. So, don't throw stones at this despicable Shirley because you, yourself is a bag of sleaze. We have more bad thoughts than good considerations. For example, when it comes to money, we will sell our brother and or sister out with a quickness. We are all murderers, and don't tell the Muckraker that you are not an executioner. You are an exceptional sleaze who rally together to slaughter peoples of other nations, as they assemble with no remorse to do the same to you. The elites are gluttons and seek strategic arrangements to keep the poor in his/her despair. Man needs a reset. A Devine lightening strike from the heavens, fused with pitch and magma from the deep is the only solution to his evil astuteness. Well, if you do not agree with me then become good, and cease from your evil doings: you nasty piece of work. Oh, just remember that I did not ask for your opinion, by all means you are here to listen to minds.

Where else, but in the American United States in the oil rich state of Texas would one think that there would have been 2,651,370 food stamps recipients in the year 2008. So-much for the Texas trickle-down effect. And another thing, how can the Texans secede with that many federal lovers. Well, as you should know, and if you didn't, here is the good news. Execution is a pastime in Texas. Governor Perry said that Texas likes to execute criminals and rightfully so. The caveat to this love for killing criminals from a conservative point of view could be far reaching, since rednecks are easily persuaded. Thus, GOP candidates could convince them that well-fare recipients in a new nation of 26 million people are criminals, and that vigilante proceedings is their only hope of protecting the upper-class from a growing welfare niche. Therefore, Muckraker has determined that secession is a codeword for execution. From my view of things going forward; it does not look good for welfare recipients in Texas.   With that bad news exposed; let's take a moment to ponder the following: *How To Kill Yourself.*

How To Get To Hell As Soon As Possible

With much respect for those of us who love our God given gift of life, I am sadden by the fact that many people who desire to die right now have not figured out the riddle to all of the prominent examples of how to kill themselves. It is unfeasible for you to be criminally charge with your death when you are dead. For that reason, Muckraker is here to make you aware of pass events and future foolishness that are at your disposal. All I ask, please do not hurt those of us who has found a reason to live.

Someone says that there have been "500,000 or so suicide deaths in the U.S.A. from 1979 to 1996". That's a very large span of 17 years or so. Well! Here is your chance to increase that number. The governments or GOP should set a 25% tax cut challenge to citizens of 1000,000 volunteered deaths each year. The congress must be exempt from this benefit in view of the fact that they are exempt from everything else that hurts hard working Americans.

For large mass suicide events that may appeal to you and the people who would like to die with you as a group: you may follow this example. Now, in 1997 in Rancho Santa Fe, California 39 members of the Heaven's Gate sect killed themselves as the comet Hale-Bopp approached earth. It is said that they supposed that a UFO (unidentified flying object) type spaceship was concealed at the rear of the comet Hale-Bopp and that this spaceship would carry their souls to wherever they think it would carry them.

Well, for this method you will need the following things that are very easy to obtain.

First you are going to need a comet. Solution: just find one, they are free, and they usually fly pass the earth all of the time. If the comets are slow in coming close enough to earth, switch to unusual meteor showers. After all, if you don't want to be here on earth with us Muckraker definitely do not want to keep you Waiting.

Next, you'll need a faith base system. This also is free. Follow the lead of the Texas religious group known as the Branch Dravidians' leader: David Koresh. If Koresh can get so-many good people to follow him, you can too. By the way, improve the hell-bound mechanism by going high-tech. Get thousands of people on the internet and execute your plans there. Southern states have a lot of anger built-up in them; therefore, they'll make good prospects. Arizona is also an extremist enclave; they even have a law about Jewish people's nose. As a consequence, if you decide to go for a visit, you may have to show your papers after crossing the Arizona border, so make sure you have it. On the other hand, instead of becoming a copycat you can just think-up a faith base system. Please contact your closet cultist for suggestions.

The next thing you will need are believers. No-o-o problem, people believe anything now a-days; the masses are looking for something to accept as true. If, whatever is being offered is immoral or evil they will practically brake their necks to get involve with it. For example, consider the fact that the GOP convinces food stamp recipients to vote against their own interest of not being able to get food stamp anymore and then they regret it. You will not have any problem finding suckers. Please, follow my advise do not go foreign, you can find all of the nitwit members you'll need right here in our U.S.A of America. Some even have PhD's. Last but not least, you will need poison. You should get a concoction that is most potent and taste good. You do not want to disappoint your believers.

Attention death seekers, Jesus already tried-out the death thing, and has been the only one of humankind so-far that has been triumphant over death. When in doubt accept his grace and you will have a different out look on life.

If the above is too much of a long drawn-out deal for you, I now introduce you to effective measures that will bring instant death. These measures will not give a death seeker a second chance. Take good notes. Jump-off the San Francisco Golden Gate Bridge when the tide is going out to sea. For group inclusion in this method, have each volunteer place chains and or shackles on feet or hands and all jumps at once from bridge. For good measure someone has already proven that bridges are excellent death makers. A determine death seeker did hit rocks as he successfully jumped to his death from the George Washington Bridge some where close to the Manhattan side of Washington Heights.

Place revolver barrel in mouth, tilt up and pull trigger. You should try it once with pistol unloaded, just incase you would like to change your mind.

Tie rope up stairs and jump down or over the stairs. Rope should be long enough for you to climb over the stairs to jump, and short enough so that your feet will not touch the floor below. It is very important to pay attention to detail when executing the method. If you do not, you will not die.

 Pretend that you are walking or jogging on the shoulder of the federal highway and jump in front of a very fast moving 18-wheeler. In or around Richmond, Texas this was just what a 33 year old man did. In some northern states and Canada big trucks may have as many as 28 wheels or more. You will not get better welcome credit to hell if you count the wheels. Your objective is to die, so do not worry about the number of wheels.

Allen M. D. Muckraker

Attention death seekers, Jesus already tried-out the death thing, and has been the only one of humankind so-far that has been triumphant over death. When in doubt accept his grace and you will have a different out look on life, and be on earthly life.

If you are defiant and still want to have a go at it, I now introduce you to smooth death. For this method, you will have to clean the garage. Cut off a piece of your garden hose. You will need this to put in the tail-pipe of your car. Make sure that it is long enough to comfortably reach into a window of the car. Go to the drug store and secure an overdose amount of sleeping pills. Close all vehicle windows before you start the automobile, and do not forget to get into the car after you park it in your clean garage and have done all preparations. You can figure out the remaining steps. Oh! This method works best for the elderly who are defiant against spiritual redemption, and would like to go quickly. By following your best judgment you will be giving the GOP a free pass, given that it is in their planning mechanism to change Social Security and Medicare as you know it. How would you like a voucher for less than the cost of your medical bills? The Democrats also have something up their sleeve too: your dead vote counts. So don't think that you will be interrupting the voting process (so assumed the GOP).

Here is my disclaimer. If you follow any of the suggestions that was discussed above you will die an irreversible death. The information that you read in this book is for entertainment only, and the writer now advise that no human's should try or act-out any of the above information. Please contact love-ones and inform them of your plans before making such a permanent decision.

Corporate America

Where else but in The United States Of America that a chief businessman/woman can be hired and be given sole charge of a very prominent business and when the company is caught braking the law, the chief-husbandman declares that the employees were running the operation by their lonesome, and he/she had nothing to do with the scandalous for the pass five years. Least to say, the law believes him/her. Where else in the world can a CEO gets paid millions to abdicate responsibility?

Where else but in a California city name Compton in The United States Of America you could find a Mayor using the city's treasury as his piggy bank and a salary to the tune of more than $700,000 plus in a city with extreme high unemployment? The FBI decided to take care of the defunct administrations future. After sentencing, the Mayor and or his accomplices will be having company everyday in their gated living rooms.

Civil Liberties

Where else but in the United States Of America in a state named Pennsylvania could you find a judge sending teenagers to jail for a fee of more than a million dollars. We may not be astounded if he is release from America's correctional comfortable institute on the good old boy system to spend his million. It may not be a bad thing to check his voters' registration card. Where Else?

Where else but in the former cradle of apartheid, in the motherland of South Africa could the police force murders disgruntled striking mining protesters on a whim? Furthermore, to justify its actions it resurrected an old law from its bigots pass, and thus charge the miners with the murders that the justice of the peace committed. The true puzzle to this conundrum in the all new inclusive South Africa is that the fanatical shooters were not only white lawmen, but included an equal niche of the all inclusive black policemen. What else?

Where else but in The United States Of America, the prison capital of the world, can a citizen invest in jailbird stocks (Corrections Corp. of America (NYSE:CXW): legal human trafficking. It have been said that the private prisons have been guaranteed 98% filling of the jail cells, and according to an Ohio sheriff' "before we start housing federal prisoners, we did not have adequate law enforcement cars and other equipments." Mississippi is competing with Louisiana to become the incarceration capital of the world. The wardens are even trying to devise a scheme of how to have the prisoners housed in his or her own house by using the infamous electronic bracelets. In one part of the State the expulsion of student from school is at an alarming high rate. The young lads feeling hopeless, then gets into trouble, and thus keeps the prison beds full. This is an effective and the millennial approach to enslave poor people. Where Else ah?

Where else but in the United States Of America that citizens are empowered by the government to kill their four months unborn kids? Where Else?

Where else but in the world of medicine especially in the United States Of America can a citizen pay for his/her Malevolent Repugnant cancer Incubation? In the real world the contributors are label: the MRI (Magnetic Resonance Imaging), the Computerized Axial Tomography better known as the CAT scan, everyone is well familiar with the X-Ray.

Yes? When the doctor tells people that they are going to get an MRI, they think that they are about to embark on a ritual of heavenly medicine. Just say MRI once.

Ooh, I love it.

Say it again M-R-I.

I say that we are about to encounter holy ground.

Well, if your doctor describes the medical procedure in real term, would you still feel good or special about getting the procedure done?

Muckraker will now describe the modus operandi this way. "We are going to expose you to the possibility of receiving a good dose of cancer by using this electrical device to see if you have cancer".

How do you feel now about that MRI?

Just for your information, the human body has lots of small God made magnets inside. Now, the guy who discovered the X-Ray did so by accident. He noticed that as he was operating a special electric type tube apparatus that special Barium-platinocyanide screen he had close to where he was working gave off some fluorescent light. Since he did not know anything about this new energy, he gave it the unknown designation of X, and added the word ray to represent light or energy. Thus, we have the X-ray: the unknown light/the unknown bean of energy.

Ok, if God made you with just enough magnetized energy particles in your body, and your medical experts excite or overload your body's capacity by surrounding it with massive manmade magnetism and ultraviolet energy light rays, What do you think that this unnatural force will do to your good health? Muckraker thinks that this intrusion could alter cell growth. That's what I think. I don't know or care what you think. Muckraker also assumes that cancer is malignant cell growth cause by unnatural forces (disease, chemical, energy, whatever) that are introduced into the body. It does not matter how many people the medical establishment test. It is impossible to know how each and every human body will react to a specific stimulus. If the FDA is so sure about some of these poisons that they are awarding us, why don't they take a sample dose of what they are selling the American public each month? Show us a little proof by eating a piece/sample of the pudding.

Where else but in the United States Of America in a state named Pennsylvania could there be a good example of the new American voters rights. The GOP in all its pump and vulgar display of democracy implemented a law to curb Pennsylvanians from voting in the 2012 presidential election. Thus, friends of the voters sue in court and wan an injunction against the law taking full effect for the near election. It was then that we also learned that the republicans also file to have an injunction place against promotion on how to get a voters Identification card. But the meat is in the pudding since republicans insist on preventing voter fraud. Given that they could not find any schemes in the democrats' registration encampment, they felt quite at home when Nathan and his bands of Strategic Alliance company   thugs, the company they hire to steal the votes were caught red-handed as swindlers of the voters Act. To save face they promptly fired them. This is unbelievable in the land of voters protection. This type of behavior makes the Chinese style of communism looks like flourishing democracies.

Where else but in the United States Of America that citizens have a choice between groping (sexual molestation at airports by government employees) and extremist Middle Easterners devastation? Muckraker has determined that having sex with ones government is a few years more loveable than embracing the sudden impact from suicide humans. Choose your outcome or stop whinge-ing.

Where else but in the United States Of America could you find a corporate person by the name of Google: an innovator? Although this person has no clue of how to build an automobile, it plans to transform it to the tune of the machine driving itself. This is an excellent concept and may save many lives, since most accidents are cause by human errors. However, there is an important issue at hand. The police is going to have a privacy intrusion party with this one. And when the developers think that they have the rights to privacy issue covered by circumventing it for the cause of safety, the hackers will than come out to ruse. This is an internet car which will most likely be sharing data with traffic-lights and the likes. This car will make the police drone program look like chicken feed. What else?   I love it.

Where else but in the State of Illinois in the United States Of America that a citizen can almost predict that every five to ten years that one of its governor's will be going to jail? Illinois is a good example, and has the monopoly on this special tradition. However, hole the phone and listen to the successful folly of Italy's finest.   If going to jail is the graduation symbol for a corrupt conservative government leader, Berlusconi is to be admired since he, the political head of the Italians have been convicted 4 times (the last time he was convicted was in the year of 2012) for shady political business practices and have never served a day in prison. Muckraker suggests that before an American citizen think about becoming politicians of the bag of sleaze that they should go to Italy for corruption enhancement classes. What Else?

Where else but in the scoundrel State of Louisiana in the United States Of America could a subordinate police officer found a recording on his police cruiser surveillance recorder that shows his boss placing drugs in a citizens automobile so that the department would collect a bounty of $40,000 to $50,000.00 they had seized from the citizen who said his family was on their way to buy a fishing trawler? Where Else?

Education

Where else but in The United States Of America could an executive of a public school allow a sports coach to rape little boys for the better part of fifteen years in exchange for football funds, power and prestige. Furthermore, when chickens comes home to ruse he/she/they hides behind the law to the tune that they had no definite knowledge of the unlawful act occurring? Can you see the glorious sign? Welcome to the all inclusive boys scouts. But like mother like daughter, or let's say it this way. A mother can always do it better than her daughter. For the reason that as Sandusky was allegedly enlarging the bottom holes of little boys at his choice foot ball camps for minors, her Majesties Broadcasting Service better known as the British Broadcasting Corporation (BBC) had one of its finest fingering and groping little girls in a choice office in the not so Great Briton. What Else could anyone expect from the descendants of the Romans? Ah?

Where else but in the United States Of America you can find a Doctor of Philosophy getting food stamps since he/she is incapable of getting tenure. The doctor only gets paid to teach one class or so.

Where else but in the United States Of America you can find that a college degree is setup to make you fail. First the student is enticed to get an expensive degree that sound beneficial. After graduation he/she now realizes that there are no jobs left in the country for the Hope Degree. The proud PHD of Hope Degree person is now confronted by the law. He/she is informed they owe moneys and must pay back their student loans. Not even a bankruptcy court can get the proud PHD niche individual out of this riddle. The single or two classes he/she teaches at the prestigious university does not bring in enough money for food. The proud PHD of Hope Degree person now gets a job as a cashier at Wal-Mart; they are just barely keeping their heads above water as he/she pays less than the minimum payment for student loans. The fascination of the college hype is now dwindling and reality not facade has settled-in.

A wholesome company made a job offer in the newspaper and also at the unemployment office. The philosopher has no doubt that his/her qualification is in sink with the employment opportunity. He/she now shines at the job interview only to find-out that the company's policy is within the fix of the government, and will not consider candidates with bad credit. Not paying your student loan is dishonoring your responsibilities.

The circle is now complete; it is currently very late in the game that the citizen appreciate that he/she has been whored-out by his or her beloved university. How do you feel? Where are all of your alumni acquaintances?

However, there is still hope. If you got the right degree that the government needs, you can work in the ghetto in exchange for your state paying all or most of your student loans. Welcome to the real world; when was the last time you voted? Are you registered to vote? Where Else ah? You better get involve with your community and tell others your story: save likeminded others from the same misery.

Social Welfare

Where else but in a Dakota's State of the United States Of America that a lieutenant governor legally kidnaps native American children and obtains custody of the kids to a private company for his financial benefits? He does this through the powers of the government social welfare/child protective program: North Dakota. Where Else?

Where else but in a State named North Carolina in the United States Of America would a sitting governor apologized for a State sanctioned ethnic-cleansing Program: better known as Eugenics (A Human selective breeding program or the said perfection of the human species by insuring that the poor and other undesirable humans genetic characteristics are sterilized. This government policy made sure that the reproduction of individuals with genetic characteristics authorize by the government as desirable were maintained as they deny the poor and lame among the masses to become extinct. The State Houses Assembly pass a bill to compensate the victims; however, the Republicans Senate's desire is to let the victims that are in their old age dye one-by-one instead of paying them remuneration. Where Else?

World Affairs/Af-friends

Where else but in The United States Of America could the African pirate's dilemma be tempered, in view of the fact that the boat capturing men of Somalia and other abetting countries now realize that the renown Guantanamo Bay prison is not for terrorist only? In reality, they are captured by brave American lawmen and are introduced to the American Industrial Prison Complex. This is the largest legal human trafficking operation. Jail stock market offers can never get any better than this. Where Else?

Allen M. D. Muckraker

Where else, but in The United States Of America could you find a man with an arm-so-strong given that as he used it one time, it wiped-out seven years of foot cycle winnings. Someone should have explained to Lance Armstrong that he had mistaken the Tour de France for the Tour de Amsterdam.

Where else, but in The United States Of America, the pinnacle of human rights, and womanlike's, would a presidential candidate declare a deviant war on women by unveiling his Big Binder of Women and a Mascot List of affluent and grassroots pussycats. Ah! Where else?

Where else, but in The United States Of America, in a Union of social justice would the obvious be ignored by millennial sleazes, that the Boy Scouts organization have been an incubator for bottom-hole sex? Muckraker now recommends that Moms send their boys to the Girls Scouts. At-least a licentious act would proclaim his manhood. Ah ha! Where else?

Where else, but in The manufacturing giant of China would a peasant be force to takeout a mortgage to get a miners job in Canada. Although muckraker may be stretching the truth a little bit. It is quite obvious that kickbacks and other unwarranted fees are serious conundrums when doing business in the real world. However, kickbacks are difficult to stamp-out in a generation of vipers. For instance, foreign teachers hired from the Philippines to work in the state of Louisiana in the U.S.A lost half of there salaries to their recruiting company. The government of the not so Great Briton paid the prince of Saudi Arabia millions of dollars to access a military aircraft contract. Thus the Chinese are no different than western sleazes; after all, they have the same compulsion to get ahead in life. And as a matter of fact, they should be commended for duping the entire world with the invention of paper money. What can you do with paper money, especially when you need a wheelbarrow to carry it? Give me an ounce of gold and I will declare something tangible. But wait because you have not heard the genius of it. You see, I believe by faith in the saving power of Jesus the Christ, thus, you and the whole world believe by faith in paper notes with dead man's heads on them. For a good demonstration of unfaithfulness in worthless-paper notes, Muckraker would like a few of you to do all of your upcoming transactions in Drachmas. So you are skeptical of what is a drachma? Ha, ha! A drachma is a unit of Greek currency. Yea, Greece money! At this point in time you can become a millionaire real quickly by exchanging some of our worthless U.S paper notes for millions of their worthless paper notes. Now, the Chinese made sure they gave us a way out of our misery when such a time comes by inventing fire-cracker, thus you now have the .38 caliber or 9mm bullet to blow your brains out when you have switch total faith from Jesus, the Christ, to worthless paper money and consequently when the system fails.   Now, to pay them back for their gift of the currency conundrum we awarded the Chinese capitalism and we seems to be winning their hearts and minds. Although communism is the equalizing forte of the Middle Kingdom (The People's Republic of China) their communist leader of apparent menial means is explained by our western news media this way: the leader's wife is dubbed an affluent diamond queen, grandmamma has over $100,000,000 and his son, a well-heeled millionaire in the executive ranks. Muckraker would like to know what happen to the communist version of a classless society within the definition of communism.

Muckraker's Folly

Where else but within the heavenly sanctum of Rome would a earthly divine father court-martial his butler for passing out secret papers, accounting for unholy acts of Grace within the papacy. Muckraker demands that his holey-ness forgive his manservant for his unholiness, in view of the fact that his wholeness was running a holey operation.

Where else, but within The United States of America, the manufacturing genesis of fairness, would a Republic-Party-conned-man or a Republic-Party-conned-woman be proven absolutely correct in all their efforts to stamp out voter fraud. The Democratic Party should be in a frenzy of joy right now, since the most recent egregious law indictment of voter fraud in the year 2012 have been the operatives of the Republic-canned-Party. Muckraker now recommends that the law initiate a search in an effort to find 78000 live kicking dead people on the GOP's voters roll. And not only that, every garbage-can behind a Republic-conned-Party registration drive boot should be check for Democratic registration forms.

Where else but in The United States Of America could the mother country of England be demagogue for letting their bankers launders billions of dollars from the Cartel druggies? Is it a bad example that they got a better piece of the action? The border fence is incomplete. Where Else?

Where else but in The not so Great Britain, the instigator of the Boston Tea Party riot in the United States Of America (due to excessive taxation) that an Olympic games conundrum with a security giant demonstrates that finally the British empire is dead. I invite our mother countrymen to follow our American lead, and throw the costly crown head over heel, out on its head. You should have given us the contract to secure the Olympic arenas and your military men would have enjoyed their period of leave as they would have avoided the wroth of sitting in unfilled Olympic benches. Come see us next time and we promise that we will not let you grovel as the West Indians did. We give you our word. We will not leave you out on a limb as we did the Cubans, Iranians, Afghans... to name a few. After all Chap, we are talking about saving our mother. As you ponders the above information, please send the prince back to Las Vegas; we're trying to get a headwind out of our unrelenting recessive none-recession. We grovel for this one. You do know what grovel means, right? Just in case you have forgotten, just ask any West Indian Cricket team member, and he'll set you straight. Ha! Where Else?

Where Else, But In a worldwide race of prestige did men loose their britches at a point in time when they realized that the Russians were the first to lunch a big antenna into space: Sputnik 1(the first artificial Earth satellite) and have it track around the earth (orbit). As a consequence, their actions caused the unfolding of a man driven rocket attack to the moon. And from that celestial invasion, we now have "one small step for man and one giant leap for Russian President Vladimir Putin" as he has out done us one more time. The genius is now the first prominent president motorized hand glider pilot Siberian white crane habitat leader. The man has actually escort a crane of birds to their habitat by leading them with his presidential Russian motorized kite.

Why didn't speaker Boehner and Nancy Pelosi have this intelligence? Our country's covert-ist has gone from giving bad intelligence to not giving any Intel at all. If President Obama had this timely information, he could have stop the Vladimir's glorious aspiration or join him, and also became one of the highest esteemed in the animal kingdom. Vladimir at this time, in this millennium has all of the animal lovers pissing on themselves with glee.

Our beloved astronaut Neil Armstrong, the first person to walk on the moon has died at the age of 82. The first U.S. woman to travel into space died at 61: Sally Ride. The nation cries out for an uplifting and enthusiastic exceptional American leadership act. After all, for conundrums in pass centuries, leaders were great in their times as they actually led their men into battle. Our modern world leaders are pusses less one: Vladimir.

Muckraker has a suggestion that does not include playing gulf. I do not know if our American president is afraid of heights, but this Holy Grail of suggestion that will rally the American people does not include invading other nations. We are not going to kill any body; therefore, the defense department is not included. They may be a bit upset, but to hell with dropping bombs on others. By the way, this test will approve the president's manhood.

Muckraker would like the president to dawn a parachute and jump from Air-force one from an altitude of 15000 feet. He will then guide himself and successfully land on the Whitehouse lawn at the point on the helipad where his Air-force one helicopter lands at the Whitehouse each time. This will make nationwide headlines, and absolutely put the republicans in a frenzy, in as much that they will wet their draws. Oh! and panties. I do not want to offend anyone; in view of the fact, that there are men in the GOP that wear panties: Log Cabin Republicans.

A Compassionate Jimmy Who Stood-Up Each Day

Where else but North America could two countries be friends? And now I would like to finally end this rant with a humanitarian story; just so that you can clear your head of the enlightenment you've just read/heard.

Jimmy was a compassionate and natured man; Jimmy McConnell was his real name. He devoted his entire life to charity, and God blessed him as he lived to be a ripe old age of 86. Jimmy had a knack for fun raising, and since he did it from the heart, he became a winner at doing so. Everyone in town knows him, and thus appreciates his goodness. At one instant he even helped his town's men with an arduous civic financial dilemma, and they cleared that pecuniary hurdle from the red and into the black. He had never once supported an unworthy cause. As loving as he was, his number did run-out, and he died a meaningful aged man's death. However, Jimmy's fun raising efforts became more astute after his death. Before the beloved members of his town lay him to rest, he answered a call to help his fellow-men and women acquire a bit more funds for a sport-plex in his town. He conjured up a plan while he was alive. It was a crude thing and no one had ever tried it before, and out of respect the funeral home rejected his compassionate enthusiasm as a ruse of last rites. Jimmy explained to the memorial servant that if they will not honor his wishes that he was going to take his business elsewhere. To their surprise and others, at the time of his wake, an admission fee of $10 was charged to all that entered, and the money was placed in Jimmy's casket as he laid there dead. The funds were his final endeavor to help finance the town sport plex. We the so-called civilized bunch have never charged for baby showers, or weddings but for Jimmy's wake his towns men felt honored to pay a fee of $10 at his wake. And so it was that, even as he lay there in his coffin, as dead as a door nail, he was still supporting his community with a righteous act.

In closing, anyone who's invited to a baby shower or potluck is expected to bring something of value to the event. On the other hand, when bidding farewell to love-one's passing, you don't expect to be hit-up for a dollar or two by a dead host, except the dead host is Jimmy. Come to think of it, this could be a genesis in its own rite. It shouldn't be long now before the fans of Elvis and Michael Jackson descends on a piece of real estate for a gathering of their resurrection. There will only be one catch to this ploy: a $50 admission fee. Jimmy McConnell was a citizen of Saskatchewan, Canada, and he once lived on top of the world. When he was alive each day he stood-up and we stand-out.

Muckraker's Folly

A Gasp From Talking Points Factory

The Spiritual

Allen M. D. Muckraker

Muckraker's Folly

Table of Contents

> The caveat here is that if two penises are assumed to be better than one, remember to latch the front door.

Prayer Meeting Quandary

Angela Gordon is everything spiritual. The energetic baby-boomer is quite active in her church and spends allot of time volunteering for church sponsored dinners to help the poor, choir practices, events that donates all earnings to a scholarship fund for the educated minded ones in her church and a social in-house women support prayer gathering for her age group of church members. After a good dose of prayer and singing, the women socialized as in getting to know new comers better, run a train on the walking newspapers and indulges in each other secrets. The little get-together brings out the human in each member, and many of the participants depends on this social niche as a balance to keep them sane, since their military retired husbands mostly works as contractors in the killing fields overseas.

Carmen is a branded speak-softly hot potato of middle age. We may take the liberty to proclaim her a closet anomaly. During the gossip session, she made an unexpected announcement to the group. I have become an instructor and I would like to help everyone in my group. The girls all bright eyed ceased all chattering and gave an ear in expectation of her offer. Carmen does not need the scoop on the group, since she is a regular at their meetings. Thus she knows all about her sister's business. As Carmen was about to speak Mildred stop her and announce that she drank allot of apple juice and the body must relieve itself. She requested that Carmen wait until she return to declare her proposal. Everyone-else now takes the liberty to have a potty break. She waits unwearyingly for their return. As they gathered, she continues to pluck the grapes from the bunch set in a saucer on the coffee table. As the last person took their seat, Erma sulkily shouts, "Well, we're all back and ready for the IQ lesson you have for us. It better be good."

In due of the fact that they just finish a prayer meeting, the proclamation was quite an eye opener for the group, as Carmen explained that she would like and is now prepared to give them sexual lessons. The girls were stunned. Angela fired a harpoon of words in Carmen's direction. "Hell no" she said, I can teach my husband all by my lonesome. The others in the group sat silently staring at each other, then Elana the chatterbox, who claims that she has place her husband on a sexual diet, grab her purse and announce that she must leave immediately for an appointment. All of the other women just moments later got into their cars and depart the seen with a swiftness.

Angela and her husband are very tight. Their marriage have been super-glued by their love for each other, as a result, they adore a healthy gossip session between them both. Angela calls her husband Bruce to give him the news.

"Hi honey" she said. Continuing with a question: How's work? Bruce, replied quite cheerfully as he was happy to hear her voice. Same-O, same-O, nothing new here: processing accident reports. Bruce works for an insurance company. He commutes 12 miles to work and back. The job is the dream of his life.

Angela responded, "Well, the girls came over today".

Bruce, "Had a good meeting?"

Angela, "Got more than I bargained for."

Bruce, "Ha! Wan…t to fill me in?"

She could not wait to get the dirt out.

Angela, a hot potato claims that she is a sex therapist. She actually said instructor.

Bruce, "I hear you. So when will she and Gibbs be giving demonstrations?"

Angela, "Don't know, and really don't care. All of the girls disappeared in five minutes after her proclamation."

Bruce, "When I was in the military it was not uncommon to hear about the wife swapping riddles. The satanic erotic's never had a good end. Wife or husbands start becoming attracted to the other party's spouses, and walla; the kids suffered the most during the divorce. One of my military acquaintances even ask for my advice on the subject. He explained that his friend was mad at him for having sex with his wife when he the husband was not present to watch. He ask me what was the difference if he was present or not present? I did not reply with an answer. Do we need more spice in our sex life?"

Angela, "What? You're already running me ragged doing it five times a week."

Bruce, "Calm down, Calm down; just checking."

Angela, "You love me?"

Bruce, "You do not have to ask honey; you know I do."

Angela, "Good! Do not stop by Gibbs today. You come straight home to me."

Bruce, "Ok, honey, deactivate the panic button. Track my move; I'll be home for more than Christmas. See you at five O'clock."

Angela, "I love you."

The dial tone sounds allowed.

Written by, Mr. Allen M. D. Muckraker ©

Be Sure, Your Sins, Will Find You-out: I

A man was getting a little poonthing in a parking lot near a club in the heart of the city of Killeen, TX. He was enjoying the pleasures of the penis and vagina as he consummates this adulterous act. Unfortunately, as he made his rounds in banging someone-else's wife, there was a tap, and a tap, and a tap, tap on the window of his car. Sadly for him it was a police officer, who then charged him with conducting licentious behavior in public spaces.

He was skillful, and could have untangled himself out of this knot, but the Omen was too powerful for him to deceive it. Therefore, or we should say consequentially and devastating for him, the officer who arrested him was his wife's friend husband. The devil never furnishes culprits with worst-case scenarios; he just showers us with the benefits. Muckraker will now therefore leave it up to your imagination to envision what later occurred between this man and his spouse, in view of the fact that, she received instantaneous information.

Written by, Mr. Allen M. D. Muckraker ©

Be Sure, Your Sins, Will Find You-Out: II.

The caveat here is that if two penises are assumed to be better than one, remember to latch the front door.

Joe loves his family. The brave heart is an American (U.S.A) fighting-man. I had to clarify which American's, since we Americans in the U.S.A throw a tantrum in acceptance that Canadians and Mexicans are also types of Americans. His countrymen sent him to kill people in a foreign country and now he is on his 14 day break. He is loyal and conducts his duties without remorse. Starving for a good draft of sex, he has grate expectations also to see all in his family. Joe's plan is to make a daring surprise for his family. The plan back fired, since he was the one being surprised. As he entered his house, there-in he found two other men. The police was called due to the violent circumstance.

Joe lived 3 or 4 houses down from the Muckraker. But I would not have done it that way. I would have contained myself as I reserve a room at the local Best Western Motel. Get on the C-list and contact a few whores and have a good time for that night. On the morrow, I would clean out the bankbooks, then put the house up for sale, assure my kids that their dad love them. Get divorce in a 24 hours divorce State, put her on notice explaining that her TRI-Care will run-out in less-than 90 days and her military ID card as well, last but not least turn-in your military quarters or put the house up for sale, or since you will be busy in the killing fields overseas just stop paying the mortgage. Do not forget the car note. Give him or her the car; change ownership completely over to the rousing spouse. Be nice, tap (in bed) the pussy-cat once or twice, then stop paying for the car to. Now, if she or he makes more money than you, you must sue for alimony.

When people desire to get a little exterior marital nucky, they should have thought about the consequences. Everyone have free will; be it their will to use it. Do not go out on the prowl shooting and rampaging because your wife leaves you. Do not mess-up your live; get a new wife or a new husband.

Now if you are a Christian and you want to stay true to your beliefs, you are now in a conundrum of the remarrying argument. It is not permitted for you to remarry if she is alive. Do not go out and kill her. Let me give you some bad advice. Pray for the witch's timely death. Believe and expect it, and it shall come to pass quickly. Everyone have free will; be it their will to use it. Why are you frowning at me? I did not ask you to agree with me. Go on; get it done. Written by, Mr. Allen M. D. Muckraker ©

Bottom Hole Sex Versus Christianity

Now, you are here because you desire *Mr. Muckraker's* opinion. Therefore, I do not need your help. This is my monkey, so let me console it all by my lonesome. Lately, bottom hole sex has been on the rise, growing at a lopsided rate in acceptance by the Caucasian's public wits. This is mostly a white people thing, and blacks are being denigrated even by the president of the United States, in lieu of the fact that most colored people find it repulsive to bend-over and experience the plagues of taking it up thee ass. In this short mocker's opinion, we will take a look at one or two good and bad recompenses of both sides of the millennial illumination.

Bottom hole sex, whether done to man or woman brings zero utility to society. On the other hand, bottom hole sex do provide lascivious eroticism to many. God give this ailing human group free will to act unconscionable. Bottom hole sex, whether done to man or woman is reimbursable with an enormous on-slot of human immunodeficiency virus (HIV), rectal cancer and other unwanted diseases. We do not have to discuss how humans obtain HIV due to their indulgence in sex. It have been discovered through medical studies that when semen (the white fluid that comes out of a man's penis that has the sperm in it) is ejaculated into the rectal canal, the body absorbs it. This aberrant amalgamation alters the functions' of the cell in that area of the body, and thus, may result in rectal malignant cell growth. Easily said, if you are a practicing agent, you may now have something growing up your butt.

I can see allot of people rolling over and would like to shoot the *Muckraker* right now, but these are the facts in raw terms. Take it or leave it, if you people keep on shoving things up your asses, one day your shit-hole will become a rotten piece of flesh.

Muckraker's Folly

Christianity has its good and its bad. If people truly fear God as Jesus recommended through faith, as to love their neighbors as themselves, this world would have been a little heaven. However, Christians have done the following: murder others: burnt them at the stake, enslaved other humans and change the word of God to fit their own benefits as well as their lust of the flesh. For example, where in the bible can one find the ordinance of a bottom hole sex man or woman of the cloth, preacher, priest or bishop?

To be a Christian you must do as the bible say or else. Paul said that for such are false apostle deceitful workers, transforming themselves into the apostles of Christ. "V14" And no marvel; for Satan himself is transformed into an angel of light. "V15" Therefore, it is no great thing if his ministers also be transformed as the ministers of righteousness; whose end shall be according to their works.

Ok! To make it plain, all bottom hole sex men of the cloth, preachers, priests and bishops are ministers of Satan. *Muckraker* now declares that if you are in one of these churches, then you are a Satanist. That's right; you have free will to do that. On the other hand, you are worshiping Satan, because the leader of that body is of Satan. Get out now; you are not and can not do any good in the devil's house. Also, if you vote for a Mormon god, you are also a Satanist. If we were in the times of Ananias and his wife Sapphira, you would be dead for knowingly supporting a god other than the all-mighty-God. You hypocrite, go fall on your knees, and repent before you have earthquake in your house.

Christianity do have disappointments. Here is a good example; miracles are not answered for everyone equally. This causes disillusionment with people, and many takes the wrong approach to combat this human blight: lack of faith. When some people pray they need to practice the art of looking ahead to receiving what was requested. You are not only flesh and blood. You are also a spirit. You can hear, see, dream and touch spiritually. Think about this though. How come all of the time you waddle in the glory of your free-will except for praying and expecting (*believing with confidence that you will get what you ask for*) that which you have requested from God will become a reality? Christianity has more good than bad baggage, even-though we have murdered many by stoning. Yes, we did. Jesus put a stop to that one by explaining that if you of the lawful are without blight please, then throw the first stone. Crucifixions are back in style; steer clear of the Middle East. Now, given that Congress and the Supreme Court does not represent the real citizens any more, If they should err, and become bound by the law, after sentencing, the Muckraker do asserts that they should be crucified. Yes, as in barbaric cross hanging. They have written the laws, and should be good examples by obeying them.

Written by, Mr. Allen M. D. Muckraker ©

The Kenworth Curse

It was August 2012 that I was driving on I40 heading eastbound: destination Woodbridge, Virgina. Where, if I was born there, I would be the sun of my brother who is my father, and my mother who is my sister. I'd just driven through what truckers call the gorge on the Tennessee portion of the highway which is well protected by the alternative tax collector: the Tennessee state highway patrol. Heads-up, I am now cautious and tiredly approaching the community of Black-Mountain in the racially prejudiced state of South Carolina. Don't blame me for referring to them as such. They were one of the states in a proud and honorable united slave holder's niche, so acclaimed a prominent senator. Here are some of the confederate states: Texas, Mississippi, Alabama, Florida, Louisiana, Georgia, Virginia, Arkansas, Tennessee, and North Carolina. In this gang of sleaze all men were not created equal.

It does not matter what color they are. For example, if they are collards (black), they articulate themselves to be racist. The blacks learned this trick from the whites. Likewise, if they are white (Caucasians) they express themselves to be naturally bigoted. These are the people who would like the return of the prosperous days of bondage. All work no play makes Jack a violent person. By the way, times have changed, and the narrow-minded niche wouldn't mind enslaving a few poor people of their own kind either.

The blacks on the other hand, would like very much to be recompensed by the children of their former masters, but the remnants are revolting against that notion. On the same token, collecting their mules promised by the government is a never ending non-conundrum that will not go away. I do not see how they live together, but they have found away.

Muckraker's Folly

Consequently, this misfortune that I rightfully owned could not have occurred anyplace else, but in South, Carolina. I, me, Tyrone am now in the Black-Mountain area, and old-man slumber is viciously knocking at my door. I was extremely happy to arrive at mile marker 67 where there is a mandatory brake-check stop test area for all commercial vehicles. There're also a few well placed parking spots for big trucks that are attuned to my liking. I've succumbed to my truckers' wits, and have decided to park the rolling giant in a vacant spot behind a dry-van. In a few hours or so he decided to move on, so I took the liberty to occupy the space he vacated.

I rejoice with my good faith and commence bedding down for the night. For good measure I start the engine to charge the battery one more time before turning in. At that moment I heard a slight roughness in the idling of the diesel engine. I dismissed the occurrence as nothing to worry about, and thus tuck myself in for the night. I awoke at 0300 hours in the morning as my body suggested that I should go and pee…pee. In good measure I decided to have a go at it.

After that exercise, I decided to start the engine and it ran for ten seconds and abruptly stopped. I then tried to start it a couple more times but was unsuccessful in doing so. Looking at my fuel gauge I now see that my fuel gauge which a few hours ago reads a bout 2/8s (which is about 45 to 50 gallons of diesel for a 200 gallon fuel capacity truck) is now hovering at or below 1/8s. I readily dismissed the notions that, 1. I had ran out of fuel. And 2. That someone had borrowed some of my fuel, and had no plans on bringing it back. Therefore, I remove the boogers from my eyes, and head-out into the elements with my flashlight in hand to identify the problem. After raising the hood (this is the bonnet: for those of you who live in the modernly not so Grate Brittan) everything appeared to be in good order. However, at a closer look there seems to be no diesel in the fuel water separator filter. I now start to believe that I had ran-out of fuel. On the other hand, I had a-lot of fuel when I parked.

During this confusion, I lost my flash light, and it is very dark. There's no way to find it in the dark. As usual, things usually graduates from bad to worst. Now, I need to call my company and tell them that I ran out of fuel. If you are not stupid, you would agree that this is a bad thing, and by the way it shows poor judgment on my part. But, before

Muckraker's Folly

I call the dispatcher to give him the bad news of how stupid I was, I tried one last effort to find the fuel.

The first thing that I the dam-fool did was to go back outside, and tap on the fuel tanks. So, here I go tapping on the left fuel tank: tap, tap, and tap... The hollow sound concurred with my fears that the tank was empty. I did the same for the fuel tank on the right side of the truck. The solid non-echoing thud coincides with my faith that the tank was less-than half full. Out into the wild I went, and upon my return I now had a measuring stick. I courageously push the stick into the right tank, and there upon by faint light from passing vehicles I measured a little-less than 2 feet of fuel. Following the same procedure I'd determined that there was less than 2 inches of fuel in the left tank. There is nothing wrong with the fuel pump. I did notice that the vehicle was slightly leaning to the right.

I now called the road repair department and explained my dilemma. He said "yep, you need fuel in that left tank". "This happen sometimes" he explains. I said "what"? His reply, "I will send you some fuel for the left tank". I was stunned. This is like a secret that no-one wants to talk about. It is a riddle that if a driver park a Kenworth big-rig on a slant/angle with 2/8 (45-50 gallons of diesel) fuel in the tanks that all of the fuel may run to the opposite side fuel tank and the truck will not start.

I would think that this could not happen in our modern age of technological advancement but it is what it is. So, the repair man came, and put some fuel in the left tank. They then prime the engine and got it running smoothly. I, the driver then move the truck about ten feet to a level area and all of the fuel rushed back into the left tank. The fuel gauge now read 2/8s plus (More than 50 gallons/about 189 liters) They, then informed me that I did not run-out of fuel, and that this happen sometimes. They then explained that they will send the company a bill for the work performed. If I was well informed about the unknown little fact, I could have avoided it, or better yet, corrected the not so understood occurrence with a piece of garden hose for zero dollars and zero cents.

Written by, Mr. Allen M. D. Muckraker ©

The Fear Of Evil Is No Contest

Being afraid is an unnecessary evil that is embedded in each individual human psyche from birth. The composition of fallen man is quite intriguing: body, mind (consciousness and thought), Soul (spiritual aspect of a person that survives after death) and spirit (the characteristical life force of a person). Fear (irrational concern, anxiety, worry, a frightening thought) is not of the Most–High (God), but the aftermath of the first Adam's ill will, and a consequential enticement from the angel of light. Why do we fear? Some may say it is due to the fact that we humans may be overcome by unpleasant feelings of impending dangers. On the other hand, many people become frighten even if there are no threats nearing them. In other words, the essence of fear may be in the mind only, or is it? In this focus, the evidence of fear is that which delineates spiritual warfare, thus the customary apprehension for life and limb due to imminent threat may appear not to be our concern: but it is.

Now, what is spiritual warfare?

Frequent characterizations may be confusing and downright self-serving to many searching for prominence. Therefore, instead of defining the actual threat to skeptical individuals I will tell you a story, and hope that you may perhaps guide your minds to grasp the physicality of spiritual warfare.

It was during the 1980s and Methuselah and Lee had just gotten married. Methuselah was now stationed at the National Training Center at Fort Irwin, California, and Lee had never traveled from her homeland of Korea or even gotten on an airplane. In her country she lived a modest life among the Buddhist but her heart was always Christian. Consequently, the struggle for her soul began in her own country, and the unseen battle raged within her sphere. As a little girl she was introduced to Sunday school, and she became committed to the foreign belief of salvation in Jesus Christ. Her father, a pious man who believes in his countries culture and teachings was stead fast in his will to deter his daughter from serving a new and foreign God. On Sundays he would stand in her path with a whipping wood as he assumed her preparations to depart for Sunday church. Lee, on the other hand, discerned her father's actions and would climb through the window of their residence, thus her father would chase her through the streets of Pusan with a whipping instrument in his hand. This would literally happen each Sunday she attempt to attend church services.

This was her world and she lived in limbo until she met Methuselah the American soldier who was not a real American. It was not easy for him to pluck her out of her mothers grasp, and Lee was not too keen on leaving her country as others who receives the opportunity to travel to the assumed land of plenty. Thus, he had to obtain her mother's permission and it was not simple, but he did what he hat to, to capture his new love and he endured.

After their deplaning at the Sacramento airport in California, a sad turn of events occurred as Lee was hospitalized due to the fact that she became ill. The event made a big seen at the airport which resulted into the hooplas of a cinema like emergency. After her revival, they took a flight to Ontario, California, the last part of their travel by air to their final destination. It was all cozy for a few months, but as usual, military life never stays typical or stable, and Methuselah was now being sent off to advance noncommissioned officers indoctrination. Future promotions are base on acquiring advance military knowledge, and Methuselah has no other choice if he desires to make the army a career but to move forward with his military training. Classically, it is the normal tide in a happily married couple being set apart due to patriotic responsibilities.

And so it was that her husband journeyed off to his duties and she was left alone in a strange land with few friends. At thirty one, she had lived a blissful life in her former years, but since she made her acquaintance with Methuselah they would go to church now and again. Thus, her yearning for the life of being Christian pursued her. Living 55 miles from civilization is never a good thing in a strange land, but her husband believed that she could hack it in his absence so he let her be. He had tried before to find a friend of her culture for in his history class he met a student of the brand and nature of his wife. He befriended his class mate and since he walked a mile or so to class she gave him a lift that was nearer to his military quarters. In an innocent gesture, his desire was that she spends a moment with his wife, and she accepted his proffer. It was his first run-in with his Lee for the clash of cultures had beguiled him. His love was exceedingly kind and welcoming to the lady, but after her departure she metabolized into a tiger of a woman, for her complaint was that he should have requested her permission before he brings a stranger to her house, and a woman at that. She willed to kill him, and he promised not to disrespect her any more.

After the momentous brouhaha, in a setting of calm, his wife made it known to him that she was quite please with her setting, and was well able to pick her own friends. It was then that she revealed to him that she had the scoop on the entire village, and the mischief of the one whom he thought a stranger was more of a blight. Lee even-though of a strong willed was hurting inside; nevertheless, she would not tell her husband in view of the fact that she dread that he would worry and the distraction would be as meddling with his military duties. For that reason, she kept all things within, and would not release it to no—one. The two were coupled in a marital bliss of oneness, and had never been apart from each other during the two years since they had grown to love their companionship and oath of promise to one-another. Methuselah's military training was a seclusion of 14 weeks, yet when he called his wife she would never tell him of the war within her mind.

Lee had become so afraid as the clutch of evil seized her that she was not able to sleep at night in her apartment, yet she said not a word to her husband when he called her from his Colorado military den. During the day she would clean the spaces within her residence, on Sundays she would attend church services in Barstow, California. When the sun goes down her life was sheer terror. She became so afraid of the night that she would watch the television with a blanket over her head covering her peripheral view. A bible sits dormant nearing the television. She had attended church but had not read or searched the bible for her salvation, and she knew not how to pray either. Needless to say, on one occasion in her deepest fear she pick-up the bible and started to read it. The more she reads or the more the scriptures were revealed to her the more the spirit of fear was pressed upon her till she was relegated to one room in the house: the living room.

One night as she reads her bible in a state of depression and fear she fell asleep, and within her world an evil spirit grab her by the throat, and it began to choke her. As she suffocates within what felt like a dream, she called on the name of Jesus. Who told her to do such a thing? At first nothing seams to be happening, and then she yelled in the name of Jesus I am God's child. The more she yell-out the name of Jesus. The less the pressure on her neck, and as she realized the there was power in the name of Jesus; she called on the name even more. Thus, in the end she saw the hands that choked her being lifted from her neck, and the demon that choked

her departing through the front door of her house. After that episode she went to sleep night or day in her house without fear. Nevertheless, the spirit of fear could not bear to be a looser and when her sister-in-law had a bad aftermath of the hurricanes she sent her kids to live with Lee and Methuselah for a season or two. The kids slept in the other room, and her nephew cry bloody murder whenever he was placed in that room; given that he asserts that there was a ghost in that room. On a specific occasion Lee demonstrated to the kid that she was taking the ghost out of his room, and she threw the thing out the house. Her nephew never had any more problems with fear again. The question is not why the name of Jesus works during spiritual war, but why don't we humans use it all the time for every thing else.
Written by, Mr. Allen M. D. Muckraker ©

The Miracle Of The Fifty Guard Dogs

We were young and dumb. As expected, we had made a very bad decision, and had now come to regretted it. Rachel and I (Bernard) was about to disembark on our first tour as a married couple madly in love with each other. As the norms of the military caught-up to us, we were no exception to the rule and it was time to move. Worst yet, the move was overseas.

Rachel had just found a good paying job incomparable to that which she was use-to and she had a sense of inner pride on the job. Her husband was already au-fait with change of duty-station repetitiveness and took his orders in stride as he prepared his wife's passport to sent off to obtain her VISA. Bernard explained to Rachel that she could stay with his sister until he secured a place in Germany. There after she could obtain dependant military travel documents be on her way to be with him in a few months. Rachel bolted, furthermore; she countered that she did not like the plan, and that she felt a sense of responsibility with her new job and would prefer to stay in the U.S. and work, as she waits for him to return.

Bernard did not fight with her over the issue and therefore, got her a place to stay and bought her pistol. The fighting-man then altered his tour of duty from serving overseas with dependant, to a shorter tour of two years without his spouse. He also in the back of his mind wrote her off as if they were actually parting the marriage, and in due time he was on his way to Europe to fulfill his obligation to God and country. Alternatively, he prayed that God would keep her safe. And it was through this stupid decision that they found-out that they really loved each other, and wanted nothing to do with any-other. To make matters worst, when he got to his new duty station family housing was readily available. As a consequence Bernard took mid-tour leave to love her, and she took weeks of vacation from her not so affectionate job to love him more. Thus, they were miserable apart from one-another.

The single family home where Rachel stayed in Barstow, California was situated somewhat in a ghetto locale. Prayer was the only answer to this dilemma.

As Bernard worried Rachel kept-up with her everyday living and never miss a beat as she goes to church, visits with friends and worked the job. Once, there were foot-steps in her yard, and then never again. The protection she prayed for had arrived in the exact count of 50 dogs. She fed them since she did not know what else to do.

The fifty dogs gathered in the afternoon, close to sunset. They stayed all night until the morning and when she departed for work they left, and when she returned home they returned. No-one dear to enter the premises, because they surrounded the house.

When Bernard returned for mid-tour vacation, the dogs disappeared and his wife never mentioned a word about the strange happenings to him. When Bernard departed the place where Rachel called home away from her husband, and returned to Germany the fifty dogs returned in unison. They surround the house each evening till morning for two years and did not depart until Bernard set foot in the yard on east white street in Barstow, California after his tour of duty was completed. The mysterious thing was that he never saw the dogs, and did not learned of the strange guardians until his wife told him the story years later. God is real.

Author: Allen M. D. Muckraker ©

Hydroelectric Turbines In The Desert

Normally Hydroelectric turbines are placed in areas where there is an abundance of water. Muckraker believes that thinking on the level of the norm is not worthy of the status of greatness anymore. This is the new millennium; an expansion of thought is required. This is the reasoning of the times. I will try to be brief as possible. Consider your town as an open oasis of sand. In or near your town there are no rivers or dams. However, you have mustered the will fortitude

Muckraker's Folly

to dig several wells. Out of these wells you have garnered all of the water you will ever need and pump the needed water into 50000 gallon tanks for public consumption. If you have already put on your thinking cap, then you would say: many towns and cities already have such water-tanks. Well good! Let's move on to the next set.

Now I want you to imagine a hole in the side of that water tank, and envision the pressure of the water escaping from the tank. To make a long story short, I will now inform you that this is the force that we are going to use to turn our Hydroelectric Turbines. I hear you saying, what happen when there is no more water in the tank? And I now reply, that's right we will not replace any water other than that which is consumed by public use. As a matter of fact, the tank will remain more or less full to its capacity. The objective of this revolutionary idea is to have the water flow through gravity back in the tank from whence it came, or into a nearby 50000 gallon tank and then back into the original water tank. Some towns and cities have more than one giant water tank. No energy should be utilized to get the water back in the tank or original tank. Furthermore, the tank must be kept full of water or at a capacity to provide continuous flow of water energy to turn the Hydroelectric Turbines.

Consider this; there are not too many smart humans in the world. Most obvious discoveries have been more than likely been discovered. Now, comes the hard part: unraveling the so-call impossibilities. A person is not smart because they can solve a calculation of calculus. A human is smart if he she figure out a good for humanity.

The Man Who Disappeared
And Reappeared In Another Place

Many fellow humans are fascinated by movies that shows wormholes *(an imaginary means of access in space-time that joins divided worlds)* and teleporting (traveling or moving objects by use of the mind/thought). For decades, scientist marveled at the subject and thus put their two cents of folly in by saying that one day it may be possible for humans to travel from one physical place to the next through wormholes and the likes.

What if I say that according to pious history that a person have been transported in like manner once before. Just as it was meaningful for an entrepreneur to discover that there was oil in the Middle East by reading the bible; it may be true to fine the answer of how to move humans from one place on earth to another without using the art of physically traveling by foot or manmade transportation by reading the bible. Of course, scientist wouldn't want to read a book that puts evolution on the shit list; as a result we may be omitting the real clues to revolutionary changes to human travel. But wait; let me tell you a short story.

There was a man name Phillip, who listened to inner voices. And it happens so, that the voice told him to go walk on the road which goes from Jerusalem to Gaza. Thus, he always listened to the voice, so, he did. As he walked on that road to his surprise he ran-into an Ethiopian eunuch. Ok! So what is a eunuch?

Basically a eunuch is a man whose pair of male reproductive gland (better known as the balls) have been removed. In olden days eunuchs were powerful men in charge of the king's house business, and most likely in charge of the harem (private accommodations set apart for wives and concubines.

Fundamentally speaking, if you have a ton-load of women at your seat of power who adores you, you do not want a man with an active dick hanging around them. Eunuchs were also priests who take care of the Pope and his business.

Ok, so now you have it, let's get back to the story.

So Phillip met this powerful man who served under Candace, the queen of Ethiopia. The man was returning to Ethiopia after worshipping in Jerusalem. The voice in Phillip's head told him to get a little closer to the man's chariot, and when Phillip did he heard the man reading from the book of the Prophet Esaias. He then ask "Sir, do you understand what the scripture say? The eunuch seems frustrated as he replied. How can I understand if someone who knows don't explains it to me? Subsequently, Phillip explained the scriptures of concern to him.

To make along story short, the eunuch was reading about Jesus crucifixion and the watery baptism of his followers. As they traveled along the way, they were nearing a source of water. The eunuch requested to be baptized and Phillip accommodated his wish if only he believed. Consequently, they dismounted the chariot, got into the water and Phillip baptized him. Now when they were done and as they were coming up out of the water Phillip disappeared. The eunuch celebrated and continued his journey. (The ritual of baptism in this context is to be amerced under water). Immediately after that encounter with the eunuch Phillip was found, or Phillip found himself in Caesarea.

Although we may not be able to pinpoint the area of the road where Phillip met the Ethiopian eunuch on the way from Jerusalem to Gaza, any road from Jerusalem to Gaza intersecting a distance to Caesarea which is presently modern Tel Aviv-Yafo/Tel Aviv-Jaffa is quite a distance to be teleported.

Allen M. D. Muckraker

Muckraker's Folly

A Gasp From Talking Points Factory

A Natural world

Allen M. D. Muckraker

Muckraker's Folly

Table of Contents

Allen M. D. Muckraker

An Interlude With Nature

Where else but in The United States Of America that a citizen can be hit by something as lightening twice. On this occasion it's the turning cloud or tornado like phenomenon.

It was during the year 2009 that I Henry encountered a mystery that was no mystery at all. Iowa, a heaven of beautiful green prairies, which clothes the land with a striking calm of human intervention. The essence of life blends with nature, and the cancer of not eating, drinking and smelling the smog which is the norms of other states is more than pleasurable. It is in this light that I see the sate of Iowa as I make my way westward on Interstate highway 80 (I80). The sixteen wheels rolling beneath me hums along in an strenuous tune as they grip the asphalt highway and compresses it further into the ground, due to the 48000 pounds of steel on the deck of the trailer. At a govern speed of 62 mph any slight incline slows the rig down to a walking speed of 45 mph or less. When the big truck reaches the opposite side of the incline all senses say that it should move faster down hill, but it does not. It defies gravity, struggles under the uncompromising weight, and moves slower than an expected speed of 60 mph and I the driver now have to push the accelerator pedal to help the truck go down the hill. Iowa City is before me, and Des Moines seems to be father and father away each time I encounter what I determined to be an up-hill. It is the weekend and my destination today is the main terminal in West Des Moines. If I can make it there, life could be better for the weekend in a comfortable place where a tired driver can relax in a room provided by the company decked-out with HBO, WIFI that works, and pleasant surroundings.

These slight amenities and desirable environment enhances the spirit, in view of the fact that I will not be at home with the kids for the weekend, and thus, I'm resigned to my imagination of having phone sex with the wife, rewarding the kids for their good or bad deeds for the week, as well as helping-out with after school assignments by phone or on the internet. My kids are not shy about stopping me on the highway for homework emergencies. I have a very good standing in the educated realm of life and they count on this as a fact of life. Because I am 1500 miles away from home does not absolve me of manly chores at the house, and this include fixing a clog sink. Yes, I can park the truck and give the wife several ideas on how to disassemble the plumbing for the sink or pay a plumber $50 to look at it, and $45 per hour to fix it. So, whatever must be done, West Des Moines is quite a comfortable place to accomplish them.

It is a clear day, the sun is beaming with light, and I can see the horizon in the deep blue yonder. As a justified backyard weatherman, just as many of us identifies our selves to be, I have determined that there will be no rain today. After pushing the scan button on the radio and selecting a choice on the dial, I became very dissatisfied with the political wrangling, and therefore tuned them out by changing bands. It was then that I heard an announcer giving an advisory on the local weather: "Look out for slow low turning dark clouds", he said. I took a peek at my surroundings and all seemed well, not a cloud in sight, and the only unusual happenings in my present environment was a screaming diesel engine under pressure to top a moderate hill. I was right on time to hear the entire announcement on the second round of advisory news, and it went like this, "lookout for slow moving low dark clouds on I80." For a second time I peeked out and surveyed my environment to find nothing of interest: no clouds, just clear blue skies.

At present there is only one social issue. I am discomforted that the 4-wheelers that are trying to run me off of the road have no beautiful girls inside: just old farts of the sexes. If you have no idea how some of our fellow drivers behave while driving on a normal day, please be advised and do not pretend to be flabbergasted. Here we go. They pass the big-truck, then they come back into the slow lane 15 to 20 feet in front of the truck. They then put their foot on the brakes, now the truck is going too slow for the job at hand. So! I, the truck driver, Man at work) tries to pass, and they realize it when the truck is side by side with their vehicle, then they speeds-up, and when I return to the slow lane behind them, they slows down again. This irritation goes on for miles and miles until God intervenes, and cause another slower fool to block them in and I gets by. They now become extremely dishearten to the fact that I have outwitted them, and they express their disappointment with my success in overcoming the difficulty they in sighted in a common manner by letting me know that I have now attain their status of number one. Their dissatisfaction is attuned in sign language with a very aggressive middle finger. So, that is how they do that; now let us get back to the subject at hand.

The sky is not only clear, but the unusualness of not even one disgruntle truck driver on the citizens' Band (CB) radio present a strange ambiguity of the moment. Everyone should know by now that anywhere on earth where there's a CB radio, you can find a loud mouth truck driver; so, not hearing one give me pause.

However, all will be made clear and comprehensible in less than a minute. As I cress the hill with Iowa City behind me, it appeared that I was out of range of all of the commotion. Things happen fast when you are on the move. It was unbelievable what I had just ran into on the opposite side of the hill. The low black rotating cloud that I was looking for was hovering in my path and in an instant I was engulfed into it. The vehicles that were before me disappeared: vanished. The temperature dropped to freezing and my windshield was overwhelmed in a sheet of ice. I quickly reduced my forward movement to 10 MPH, then to about 5 MPH. If it was not for the windshield heater I would not have had a small clear gap at the bottom of the windshield to see the white lines on the road which appeared to be less-than 10 feet in front of the truck. I can now clearly hear all of the loud mouth truck drivers on the CB radio on the opposite side of the highway screaming about our dilemma. Out of my peripheral vision on both sides of the truck the lightning announces its presence. The lightning is not a nice thing to see up close. Out front in the deep darkness, there appear to be little balls of rolling lights. I made-up my mind that I was not going to stop; furthermore, if I do stop, where do I park? I could not see off to both sides; the only assurance I had were checkered lines in the center and a solid line to my right. When I emerged from the other side of this mess, I chose a safe place to park. I did not have to worry about any traffic, because there was none behind me for miles. I unseated myself, thank God for his good mercies and then inspect every inch of the truck for damages, and there was none. I man the wheel and continued the mission; if I do not drive, I will not be paid. This is not a job for the fainted heart.

Surprises are facts of life when you are an over the road driver. Little things upsets and aggravates others, but since I've endured a heavy dose of 20 plus years of the military nothing bothers me too much. I usually just take everything in stride, and find solutions for occurring situations. My chosen career was in the aviation field, but after joining the force they kept on giving me reenlistment bonuses, so I followed the money and lived a hard life. Even if not too much amazes me, there is always someone or one group of people on this retched earth who gives me pause, and such a liked occurrence revealed its self around the Nolensville, Harker Heights area in Texas on this occasion. I guess a good theme would be, when in doubt save your ass and no one else's. I am not as wise as many. I do have a bit of education. It was created on the stepping stone walk of life. You know it. First I finish high school, then community college, then undergraduate studies: I never completed my masters; still have about 3 to 4 courses left. I make good decisions; I think so, and yet again most of the world's horrific conclusions are made by those in the highest status of the educated realm. I call them dunces with a diploma. On the other hand I do not know the status of this mob of drivers, but they sure looked like the affluent type.

And so it was that I was headed westward, homeward-bound on highway 190 after a daunting week of driving for a living. Turning to the direction of home after a southward plunge on I35 is always a pleasant feeling that overwhelms the three persons' of the human kind: the body, the soul and the spirit. It is compulsory by nature to have a place call home. Thus, if a man roams the earth for a life time, the intervention of death involves an infinite home of some sought.

It was about 4:30 in the afternoon and my fellow drivers in their 4 wheelers were jockeying for real-estate on U.S Highway 190. No driver on the highway can occupy the same piece of asphalt and this flock of steering turning scalawags displayed an intent to do just that, but I kept my cool and let them have their way. Nevertheless, if they were hazards to good driving, then nature intensified the situation with a stoning from heaven, and the twister swooped down directly on the highway.

The hail stones were so mighty and powerful that a block of ice rake havoc on the hood of the Peterbilt truck in such a way that the company change it when I return to the terminal. Even more alarming during this natural commotion, the skies remained partially clear. This in itself was a miracle because all of the cars on the road at that time (about 10 to 15 or more did an unusual thing. They took refuge under the bridge, but not just portions of the bridge off of the road, but the entire span of spaces under the bridge on all four lanes east and westbound. Therefore, traffic movement came to a complete halt and no one was going anywhere.

These drivers were scared shitless in such a way that a highway patrol had to force them out of their presumed safe places from under the bridge in order that other traffic could pass. After the unforeseen natural intrusion, I man the wheel and continued my journey home. There is no place like home. Thus far, in the year 2009 nature had wagged its tale at me twice, and I did not like it, but there is another dance in my fortune before the year runs out: Oklahoma.

Oklahoma, a victim of the Louisiana Purchase of 1803, where The United States purchased a large track of land from the seller: France. Isn't it amazing that ne'er-do-well-ers from Europe just walk in on a nation of people, lay claim to their property, come to a decision that they own the land, and have the gall to sell it to another of their own accepted astuteness? Would it be inconceivable for Native Americans to challenge the purchase of Oklahoma from the French? If I was not a dunce, I would determine that this sale has a smell of dead fish. In light of today's millennial thinking, you can't just walk into a man's house, claim his belongings and announce a yard sale. Now-a-days we call that home invasion. But, I have a hunch that the Native Americans will never ask for the return of Oklahoma, due to the fact that it is curse by a pathway of tornado alleys. They knew it 500 years before our arrival, and it would be disrespectful to try to pawn it back off on them. Thus, let me share a pass encounter with the beastly thing. My destination on the day of the occurrence was an address on Sohna road in Oklahoma City. I overtook Dallas, Texas in ample time to miss the morning traffic; therefore, I'm in good spirits. The only concern in the back of my mind as I make my way north on I35 was that I may be overweight. Most of the times when I fuel-up in Waco, Texas I usually top off the tanks, and today I did just that, but with more than 200 miles to the scale, and burning fuel at a rate of 6.75 MPG, the 200 pounds of fuel will disappear in no-time. For that reason, I should not have any trouble passing the Oklahoma scale. As I track north it was apparent that Oklahoma City had a bit of darkness over-hanging its urban satellites. The radio announcers on the stump were giving a minute by minute spill of the entire weather situation. To my fortune, the news was not good. The evil thing had now entered into the city and reports being sent in to the radio announcer by eyewitness emphasized an ongoing mayhem as the twister bounces from one path of the city to another. I calculated that the path of the city that was in the natural uproar was further east, so I proceeded on my northward track. That decision was a very bad choice, and as I plunge northbound on I35 the wickedness of nature lied directly in my path. I had missed it by less-than a minute. Glancing to my right, it was quite apparent that two drivers had just extracted themselves from their overturn truck and have found it well-suitable to sit on the same embankment with their upside down truck. All of the road-work equipments were uprooted from their posted areas as they littered the highway. The Oklahomans did not parked in the middle of the highway as the Texans did; they knew better. About a quarter of a mile up the road, a victim of the hour surveyed his car windshield which had a bull's-eye smash, cause by flying debris. He appeared to be more-than confused, and act in a manner as though he was struck by lightning. I am not going to ask why I was saved from this disaster; on the other hand, I will be thankful that I was. As an over the road truck driver; I will not be paid if I do not drive. After observing the sad faith of my fellow Oklahomans, I manned the wheel and head to my delivery rendezvous.

There Is Enough Water in The United States
To Cover Every Drought Area
In The Nation:
The Replumbing of America

Ask any U.S American what occurred on 4 July 1776 and they will be all bright eyed, as they proclaim their versions of Independence Day. How rightfully so, any version is accepted gracefully, as long as the tyrant evil long out-stretched tax hands of the king and queen of England is deposed from their pockets. After an actualization of independence, the struggle for good became the heartbeat of the new nation, and the superiority sort after did not entailed a man made noble who berates and robs the deprived of their pride and will to succeed. Our greatness is not a spike in how many citizens become wealthy in a decade or so, but an occurrence of established public good. Our nation's irrigation system should be considered an improvement in our national security endeavor. If half of the country is always devastated by floods and drought, then our prosperity is at risk, and so goes our worldwide influence.

Thus President Eisenhower foresaw the greatness of the country with a well developed transportation system, not only in ease of military equipment maneuvering, but also as a corner stone to a thriving public good in the commercial sector, due impart to a highway expansion program. The hypocrites of his day could see no farther than their nose, and disappointed him as they first rejected his highway development agenda. What would our status in national output be today if we did not have a federal highway system? A proposal of such a public good would be rejected by The Republicans if there were too many small contractors benefiting from such government expenditures, and the Democrats would rebuffed it due to the fact that the well-heeled among us would get the better part of the deal. This is how the parties in our present political system explains that projects cost too much. The most important object of such arguments should be that the cost factor does not matter when it is time to invest in what makes us great. Nincompoops along both lines of conviction will hole fast to their political ill wills; inapt to the national utility in question. Consequently, absolute emphasis should otherwise be place on fraudulent manipulation of the financial mechanism which supports such public good.

Moving the Mighty Mississippi

Just as the federal highway system made us a great profitable economic force, and a nation of one people familiar with our country; it is inconceivable that there would be arguments among us that moving a yearly overflow of water from the mighty Mississippi and its tributaries and other rivers would be disadvantageous to drought stricken States such as Arizona, Kansas and Texas. The blessings would go even further given that those States that braces themselves for the yearly floods or whenever the torrent thus comes, the waters would be diverted to dried-up tributaries such as: rivers, lakes and streams in areas where the rain fall is well below the minimum due to growing shifts in millennial weather patterns, acts of God and other concerns.

So the motivation here is quite simple. If Libya in Africa can make a man-made-river with 13 feet wide pipes beneath its desert from subsurface aquifers in the Sahara to Benghazi and Tripoli, then we can move all excess water from the Mississippi and the Missouri rivers along with their over-flowing tributaries to Arizona, Texas, Arkansas, Kansas, Oklahoma and the likes where the rain fail to fall in adequate proportion for farmers to be productive. The benefit to such an actualization would be no more flooding of resident's home along the mighty Mississippi and the Missouri Rivers, thus billions of dollars saved in benefits to tax payers and other concerns. The project is a job multiplier.

How To Do It

There will be much opposition to this plan, since in present day America; it is the business of some charlatans amongst us to oppose even the endowed duty and goodwill of the federal government. So, here is my proposal to avoid hypocrites. The Federal government would build a 20 feet wide waterway underground, adjacent to the federal highway system, US highways, along side railroad tracks and places where feasible such as lands next to electric power-lines crisscrossing states. This put the threat of eminent domain (The authority of governments to take private property) and the environmental worshipers' challenges to rest before these doomsday exaggerators spread their ill-wills to the masses. There is nothing else on earth that is more environmentally unfriendly than a highway, and placing an invisible river next to it could increase no more harm to the environment than there already is.

The states would then, figure out how to get the water to the necessary rivers, lakes and tributaries. They can work with NASA and The National Oceanic and Atmospheric Administration (NOAA) to chart which rivers and tributaries flow where and develop a national irrigation system that is not only dependant on pipes but also the use of nature's creeks ponds and lakes. To explain it in simple terms, they would pump (solar water pumps) water from rivers into creeks which naturally runs into lakes, ponds, connected by manmade pipes when necessary until the waters reaches the farm lands or access to farmlands of drought stricken states all over the nation of the U.S.A. If the states have their heads up *"their don't know how to get it done"*, then the water is sent on its way to other states that have conjured-up the will power and have develop the means and ingenuity to get the water to their drought stricken farms. The politics of that state will be left up to their voters to censure or fire their public representatives.

There will be no time spent on those inhibiters who just aspire to make a name for them selves as they stir-up public sentiment: the environmental clunks, the republican and or democratic stooges or anyone who objects. No objectors (***lobbyist***), no stupid jingoistic citizens will be tolerated; the government should go **Mao Zedong** on this one. Our leader did declare war on a nation of people that had nothing to do with hurting us. The outcome was that we appear as fools to the whole world as we spend billions over-seas while our citizens go hungry at home. Now! It is time to declare war on drought. The end result concerns our nation's survival.

No eminent domain issues need be considered, just get the 20 feet wide pipe in the hole on federal lands, cover it up and move on. Some tributaries, lakes, rivers and over-used aquifers may be recharged directly from the irrigation source without pipes entering private lands and such water reserves. The designers can use satellite technology to map creeks that will carry the water to replenish such natural reservoirs: aquifers, lakes and basins. When these aquifers, lakes, basins are up to par in water capacity, the spigot at the source shall be turned off.

There Is No Cost Factor

A project such as this proposed does not cost, but save in human lives and amplifies national productivity. Therefore, it is not how much does it cost, but what are the savings? To get the dollars out of the argument, let's assume cost savings of $50 billion. We have spent more than that over time (since the nation was conceived) on repairing riverside disasters. Each year many enclaves, towns and cities get flooded, while other agriculture lands grow arid. The United States is more than 200 years old, and this sort of development should have been our long term plan for water productivity from the conception of the nation. I firmly believe that there is an adequate amount of water flowing in the United States each year to make our lands look like spring all year round. We should expect the present flux in weather pattern for the foreseeable future, as long as we keep fossil fuel as our main source of utilized energy. Listed below are good examples of savings provided by this proposed Nation Flood Water Irrigation Project.

Flood Water Irrigation Project Savings

1. Save human lives and avert increases in flood insurance
2. Save jobs and creates employments
3. Necessary infrastructure improvement
4. No more flooded homes along the Mississippi or other rivers
5. Ease river dwellers stress from such disasters
6. Prevent disease out brake due to such catastrophes
7. Prevent farm lands top soil erosion from acts of men.
8. Reduce contamination of local public water supply by such river overflows.

9. Stop or reduce human and economic type avoidable water disasters in the regions along the river.

10.   We will not have to blow-up the levies to save cities down range by creating a disaster for others as we flood them out of their only means of existing subsistence (Fire executives and managerial engineering staffs for such convoluted ideas and inadequate plans to deal with floods).

11.   The accumulation of good outcome from a national endeavor such as this proposed project will certainly overwhelm the negatives.

Conclusion

A do nothing approach is a warrant for future tragedy in the regions where the mighty Mississippi and its tributaries devastates communities. If we as a nation believe that the United States of America is to survive longer than all other nations on earth, then a lack of will to improve infrastructure is a definite formula that will assure our appointment with catastrophic failure. There is a good example of what an irrigation system can do for our nation's health. To study the outcome of a partial nation rural irrigation success, we should look no further than California and its agricultural successful lifeline hinged to an artery of water call the Colorado River Aqueduct. Without this successful effort, vegetables may not be available nationwide all year-round on our tables.

It is becoming increasingly evident that a national management of fresh water is necessary due to while swings in global weather patterns. As such uncertainty abounds, the yearly supply of water received must not be allowed to return to the sea unexploited. Advances in satellite technologies can do the mapping of national rivers and tributaries that are able to accommodate the yearly excess waters from the mighty Mississippi and its tributaries. This method of water redistribution can best serve the nations interest for the greater public good. Thus, farmers will not have to sell their cattle's due to lack of water in areas of the country where less than adequate precipitation is a prevailing symptom. If there is no rain no grass will grow. Farms then have to truck in water, and hay to feed their herds of cows. It becomes evermore expensive as fuel prices increase to maintain hundreds or thousands of animals. Lastly, consider the humane utility: no more devastated communities' etcetera, etcetera and etcetera. Let's not gamble with our waters as speculators and banks have done lately with multiple economies. A national irrigation system is a must, and the time to start our success to a better future is not later but now.

Author: Allen M. D. Muckraker ©

Magnificent Earth

What do we really know about our planet earth? There are many things we accept as true, but they are not as accurate as we think them to be. As you read this short brain rambling please keep an open mind; since, what I am about to say may be bewildering or quite the opposite of what you have come to know as the veracity of everyday life. It took a long time for us to accept that the earth is round. Let's take a look at some of the most recognizable elusions that we hold dear to our heart as infinite truth. Human's first misunderstanding of earths primary elusion is the notion that we can standup on all points of the earth. We may lay-up or stand-out at certain points on the earth, but we cannot standup relative to the establish direction of up on the earth. If you try to stand-up at specific points on the earth there will be nothing underneath your feet.

Where or which way is up? One day at work while at lunch I ask a fellow worker the simple question of which way is up? This person is what we may identify as an knowledgeable person. This individual stood speechless in his tracks and actually thought about the question. Several minutes later and no answer to my request, he explained that I was trying to trick him. Assuredly, this is not a trick question. There's no reason to be baffled by this simple subject. If you are seated at a desk and I request your attention by asking you to look up, you will unequivocally raise your head to look at me. This is not the up we are concern with. Our concentration is empathically directed towards the orientation of the area atop and below the uneven rocky sphere we call earth. I say Gravity surely does not reveals which way is up. It's most significant ploy is to place whatever is above or below it to a point relative to its subduing force. I know you understand the explanation of falling to earth. Now welcome to the idea/reality that all of the people in Argentina and Chile are practically walking upside-down. Therefore, how could they fall down? If they slip, they would be pulled back into the grasp of the earth by gravity through its unwarranted force. By all means of reality the fallen victim or victims felt the crushing effects of a miscalculation; consequently, the Argentineans and or Chileans thought that they fell-down, but the reality is fact that they fell-upwards.

If we take the word up literally and seriously as we humans determine it to be, up is where the North Pole is. Therefore, the only people and animals that are standing-up or almost standing-up are those who live on top of the world at the North Pole. So, we may now consider the thought of looking up. We do not have to raise our heads to look up; we must turn our head or entire body to the north. This is the absolute truth; there's no way around it. North is up, because we humans have instituted it as so.

This brings us to another perception that the sun rises in the east and sets in the west. This is false. The sun appears to come around from the east (an effect cause by a spinning earth). The sun has never once traveled over the North Pole, except for the time of Noah's flood when the earth turned upside-down, and all hell broke loose. It is absolutely impossible to look up at the sun, because the sun is nowhere near up. The solar system is an imaginary Frisbee and the sun sits in the center of that Frisbee.

There are many rocks like objects that revolves (The revolution of the objects around the sun may not be even) around the sun, and one of them is called earth. In our solar system the sun stays put; it does not move. God has an invisible anchor on the thing. If the sun moves; we are S.O.L. As humans, we walk on the side of the earth's surface, and in view of the fact that we have determined that the north-pole is up and the south-pole is down, we have consequently established a top and a bottom to the earth. The earth is not a perfect sphere as a ball with no distinct features of top, bottom or sides. For example: Reference these landmasses: Alaska, Canada, Chukot (Russian territory) and Greenland in the extreme northern hemisphere are dissimilar to landmasses of Argentina and the Island of Alexander near the South Pole. Therefore, when we are in motion, we are either moving up, down, across or at an angle to up. With that being said, we may either walk up, walk down, walk across or at an angle relative to the sun, and to look directly out at the sun we must raise our heads.

OK, try this. Line your body up with the earth by laying down flat on your back, and "walla" you are now looking out at the sun. We can only look out at the sun, because the sun is more across from the earth than above it.

At this moment in time you may be confused; thus, I have more puzzlement to bestow upon you. Here is another one. It is also almost impracticable to be on the surface of the earth and walk away from the sun. However, for this idealism/reality you have options. Remember I ask you to lie on your back and look out at the sun? Do that again; now, roll over on your face and walk away. What happen; you had the same results as the last practical exercise? Take a look at some of these options. You can walk into a cave, but you cannot be standing upright when you walk into the cave. The cave must be angled towards the vertical center line of the earth. Ha-ha, you think that you can walk down a hill/mountain and be further away. You may be further away, but you are still on the earth's surface, and what you have just done was to angle yourself away. Now, stop right there, lay on your back look out at the sun, then roll over on your face and walk away from the sun. You can dive into a body of water, or fall into a well or mineshaft! These work better (Please don't try any of these at home without the proper safety devices; death may occur). While you are in the thinking mode, get a grasp of this. Why don't the statue of liberty in New York and the Eifel tower in France not falling down, since they are actually on the side of the big rocklike ball we call earth?

My final challenge is to bestow the enlightenment that the sun is never directly behind you save for a few instances and physical area on the globe. For example: You can face the east at dusk, or face the west at dawn (in the morning when the globe is spinning from west to east), and at midday, lay down flat with your face towards the ground and your back to the sun. The next portion of this exercise is the vacation that you need to plan, since you must be at latitude zero, and if you do not live at one of these places in this list, then the sun is not directly behind you: Guinea, Gabon, Congo, Uganda, Kenya, Somalia, Indonesia, Nauru, Galapagos Islands, Ecuador, Columbia, brazil, In the ocean at latitude zero. Take your pick from one of the vacation spots or fine a tanning spot somewhere else at latitude zero to get the sun directly behind you. Do not forget to lay down, turn around and look at the earth face-down or you will sure to be disappointed on your return home. This entire read is a thinking exercise. On the other hand, I know that someone out there will have the gull to try this; therefore, be safe in your endeavors.

With a good understanding of the latter you will now understand why Alaska and northern Canada have so much twilight and darkness because of the earths wobbling (the top and bottom of the big ball called earth moves back and forth over-time which gives us seasons). The closer you are to the equator (center of the earth) the less dramatic the seasons. Farmers may now plant and harvest year-round. Believe it or not, we actually live on a wobbling spinning piece of rock. This brings me to another topic: Stellar rocket Launch Windows, but we'll leave that argument for another time.

In conclusion, we have established earth's relative position to the sun and the fact that it is unattainable for us to look up at the sun. It is also clear that according to human thought and acknowledgement that up is where the North Pole is, and if you have the desire to stand-up you must go to the North Pole, or lie-down on your belly or back with your head towards the north pole. Every person in Texas stands-out when walking, because the state of Texas is on the side of the earth. A comparable offset or opposite is to have the desire to stand-upside-down, for this elusion in a real world you must go to the South Pole. To be upright relative to up (The North Pole) at the South Pole you must stand on your head.

Written by, Mr. Allen M. D. Muckraker ©

Muckraker's Folly

A Gasp From Talking Points Factory

True Military Hiccups

Allen M. D. Muckraker

Table of Contents

True Military Hiccups

Be Sure To Follow Your Own Advice

Where else but in The United States Of America could a former fighting-man be so at-eased as to share some of his wanton military life's experience with his countrymen.

It was now the nineties and not too long before that I was transferred from Fort Irwin California in the grand old U.S.A to mingle in the German arts and culture. When I arrived in Freeburg Germany my battalion had also just recently returned from Gulf War One. As a buck sergeant I was assigned to C Company and my potential official duties was to become the platoon leader's gunner on one of Uncle Sam's finest piece of equipment: the M1 tank. Being assigned to a class room type environment at the brigade's Opposing Force Academy at Fort Irwin, California was an affluent undertaking; however, I was now back in the company of the regulars and my gunnery skills were not up to the level of the seasoned warriors. Therefore, I was reassigned to the battalion's

Headquarters and Headquarters Company, and was given six men and a few trucks. As bad as it may sound, it was a good place for reintegration, since my squad was part of the Support element that supply the guns with the needed bullets.

The reunification of East and West Germany started in 1989 and was completed by October 1990 and a few years later, it was the time for base closures and the establishment of the GI's (the soldiers') dream: open post. For you none military kind, this means a military post with no gate guards, and to bring you into the true enlightenment of the GI, this means a free flow of women and wine on post. No more signing in and signing out of friends; I think you get the picture. The first time the band was lifted I was even amazed at the sight; it was as though a second East Germany had fallen. There were Germans everywhere on post and every GI got him a girl. The party was so extensive that they slept on the sidewalks all night, since the spirit within them held them at bay. I was not able to join the wanton crowd since I was now a married man, but I did not need license to go out at sunlight to see the hangovered glee bunch which took possession of the lawn, and other spaces as they spend the night. I was the battalion's orderly for that night. It was a happy environment; the stuff adventurous recruits dreamed of as they pitched their will to be in the company of the likes' of Uncle Sam.

It is quite evident what manmade spirits can do to humankind. I had experience the brunt of it on a peaceful occasion. My fellow sergeant invited me to his house, since we worked well together and found it pleasant to be in each others company. He had two beautiful kids and a marvelous heifer of a wife. He invited me to his house, where I spent the night. Surprisingly, he'd turnout to be quite a bibber, and when he was drunk, he showed his dark side and did even called me a nigger at one time. His wife scolded him for it. I forgave him since he was displaying his true upbringing. He later drank himself into oblivion and he lost his career as a soldier. I felt sorry for the wife and the little ones.

It is now Friday and the GI is quite poised to let off some steam on the weekend, for the toils and pressures of military duties had been difficult during the week. All of the men of the Fourth and Sixty Seventh (4/67th) Armor battalion are in formation. They are in good spirits, for the wit of German girls and

German beer awaits them. The battalion Commander tells us how important we are to America's goals, and that we are the best in the business in keeping the world safe. We all looks' at him as if he is a crazy man, and wanders when will he be finish with his speech of rubbish. Know one really wants to hear anything about America's ambassadorship at this point in time, and since we are all in one mind, we think dearly that he should leave that ambassadorship stuff up to the party poopers in Washington. We relished the ending of his speech and he now calls on one of his commissioned officers' to dose us with the battalions' weekend safety briefing. He speaks.

"Good afternoon men."

We responded in one roaring voice of more than five hundred men, "Good afternoon Sir."

He smiles, because he understood our pain in the fact that we had to stand there and listened to the Battalion Commander and his Sergeant Major as they tell us how much they love us. In our minds, we are wandering why don't they quickly advance home to their wives and kids and display some of the same love they are giving to us as soon as possible.

Muckraker's Folly

The safety officer, "Men, wear your seat belts and drive safely; do not leave your cars on jacks."

The GI most often drives a clunker and when it clunks out he jacks it up, and being frustrated with the mechanical riddle, sometimes he leaves the thing on its' mechanical jack for weeks. This becomes a hazard to anyone nearing it.

He continues. "If you are going to have sex please wrap it in a good sexually proven device? If you have and emergency call the battalion or your unit's orderly. Don't drink and drive. Get yourself a designated driver. Have a good week end; he calls the battalion to attention."

The men are release for the weekend. Needless to say, Monday morning bright and early the safety officer was also included in the brawl of men stopped by the police and found in violation of DWI infractions.

Author: Allen M. D. Muckraker, Copy rights reserve ©

Black Market Cigarettes

It was a lovely Saturday and there was not a cloud in the sky. Having nothing planned for the weekend, I settled down to play a game of risk with the other barracks rats. Whenever the words black-market is mentioned, the world thinks of men in black suits and the criminal élites commanding the trade. However, the underground traffic is presently right within our midst, and if we just lend an ear or an eye or two, we would be able to hear, see and even feel its existence. For instance circumventing the tariff emplaced on a pack of cigarette in the state of New York is as simple as it gets, and you would be dubbed a criminal for buying untaxed rolls of shredded tobacco.

The military is a place where limits are quite the norm, and although the worriers do not relish such intrusion in their personal lives, they expects it due to the closed martial culture. There is no end to the list of people who get caught selling none-Taxed military goods. For instance, a situation wherein a close friend of my spouse got into a spate of desire gives a good example of the act in question. A soldier from a certain military Criminal Investigative Department apprehended the spouse of a soldier as she dealt in the underground trade of rationed military goods such as mayonnaises, cigarettes and the likes. It was quite shocking to the investigator when she announced that he was quite hypocritical in his doings since he was causing grave trouble for her and her husband when his wife was a regular indulger in the band practice. In disbelief, he launched out to seek-out the truth, and at the end of the hunt, he found his wife vigorously dabbling in the forbidden business, and he was disheartened.

And so, during the nineteen eighties when the Soviet Union was characterized as the foe. I was a defender of the free world, and to my delight, it was a marvelous merriment to be stationed in the German party heaven of Manheim. More often than not American goods are tremendously valuable commodities in many nations that accept the hospitality of our military presence, and the GIs (soldiers) usually run a muck of the system since they are no kin to piety and were most likely deprived in status and culture as they bridge the eventful gaps of life's realities. On the other hand, I the outcast of the GIs customs was borne in what Americans call a third world nation, and having nothing was the norm, so the inspiration of making a few bucks from a guarded trade was far beyond my nature since the Leavenworth criminal palace of military braves was never a destination of my liking. Living with scoundrels was an eye opening event, and a bit of a teaser, thus the insatiable infirmity was ingrained in the best of my warring comrades, and many try their hands at the viral thing and was found wanting. I never could understand the choice concept of instant gratification to gain a few American greenbacks (dollars) for the alternative award of six or more months of hard labor, and an end to a gratifying career. Anyway, many fell into the soup and the amalgamation of status range from the lowest of privates to a penetration into the heart of the ranks of the commission officer's core. The knack of challenging prevailing acceptable social standards is ingrained in the mind of all humankind, and not even Uncle Sam was able to stop the torrent wave of adventurers in its ranks. Nevertheless, he has a scheme metered out in the human ballet of seekers to get his man, but it is confusing at times when the wrong doer is none other than he who should be prosecuting violators.

And so it was as I had completed my game of risk, in walk the S2 Staff Sergeant. For good measure lets name our S2 Staff Sergeant Benedict, after the order of Benedict Arnold who had a bit of revolutionary disloyalty to America during the war which occurred some where about the time from 1775 to 1782 or 83. Ok! To bring those of you who knows nothing about the military into the military realm for your understanding of our culture, if I say KGB you have now snapped into the correct frame of mind. So, for our analogy of this read, the S2 detachment (personnel) in our battalion is our little KGB detachment. You screw-up on unit's intelligence or anything which falls into this category and they will have your hide. Furthermore, this office is the one that divvies out the ration cards to all members of the units, and they monitors' its usage. They are the real deal, and once upon a time I had a little interrogative session where I was all by my lonesome in a room of investigators yelling at me. They were investigating an incident in which my unit's members had indulged in a bit of sabotage; the dealings of which I knew not. Nevertheless, in their eyes we were all scoundrels so I received the same dose of the poison they were divvying out to the other fearless comrades. To their dislike, I held my ground and could not be swayed, since waterboarding was not yet legal. If it was, we would have been in deep shit and would have told them whatever pleases them.

Allen M. D. Muckraker

I know Staff Sergeant Benedict quite well, and he appears to be a man of reasonable character. I am not all alone in this world by my self, and I am reasonably sure that if you caught the police stealing from Wal-Mart you would be rather confused also. A Judge in a fairly large state in the union of the United States was caught in the evil of sentencing juveniles without due process to the lockup for kickbacks. He was dealt an ounce of his own judgment, and by far end-up an unhappy camper. So, if other men of the law have fallen into the soup, it may be also difficult for the hands of our dear uncle, Uncle Sam that is; to be sanctimonious. Anyway, to make a long story short, there I stand in the hallway cornered by Staff Sergeant Benedict who would not relent on the possibility of me illegally using my ration card in acquiring some cigarettes for him to quench his smoker binge. In all reality, I was scared shitless, and could only see the bars of Leavenworth in my future, if I complied with his wishes. After a lengthy corroboration of no's he finally leave me be, and he departed my presence in disgust due to my stern insistence on a fixed reply of no. How do I know when a law man desires a bit of unlawfulness? On that note, considering what I know to day about the human cravings for dried shredded tobacco leaves, I should have bought him a pack and gave it to him as a gift. At least that would have been somewhat legal; excluding, that the act still could have run a muck of the Uniform Code of Military justice, since he was twice my senior.

I hope that you are enjoying your read.

Written by Mr. Allen M. D. Muckraker, ©

Titi Bar Confession

Hypocrite Symons was a good and decent sergeant; a family man he was. He is a member of the team on this mission, and is the culprit of our woes amidst the saying: follow your best judgment. Our duty was to train and evaluate the Mississippi National Guard and our present destination is the Mississippi town of Grenada. There is an armored unit that is home base in that region and the tank combat gunnery skills test must be completed before a single shot is fired. So, as military regulars my team saddled up and do what civilians normally does not do; leave our families behind for the relevant notion that our cause is for the good of the nation. The drive up Interstate highway I55 was calm and peaceful, and we kept ourselves content and merry by rehashing old soldier's jokes. As we stop to visit the restroom I did not have to go so I sat in the van.

During the potty brake Sergeant James and Sergeant Murphy struck a deal with a Subway sandwich store, and it was a point of sale arrangement that they had determined they could not refuse. Upon their return with the lofty bread and twice the amount of meat than usual, I felt a bit envious; furthermore, they explained that it was quite a bargain and two for one at a meager cost of $5. My mouth watered as the digestive saliva between my cheeks beckons me to ask for a piece of the breaded sandwich; however, my pride said no, so I in turn gravitated my interest to the horizon and the luscious meadows betwixt the farm land and pine tree forest patches. Then they orchestrated another iteration of psychological strike on my meagerness as they explained that assimilating in the Mississippi culture would be good for us as we meet the people and spend our moneys in the local stores during our travels.

I tinkered with the notion that too much free stuff in these modern times could spell trouble since the days of free things are all gone and a price must be paid for even the accomplishment of good deeds. My inner spirit encouraged me to leave them be and let them enjoy their perceived good fortune. 45 minutes later into our journey Sergeant Murphy developed a rash of stomach pains and the enigma seems to take hold of Sergeant James also in as much as he could not hold his bowels. The driver polled over at a private business to assist with their emergency and the 100 yards dash was accomplish in lightening speed as they heads for the potty. Each benefactor had one more two for one Subway sandwich remaining. By the time we arrived at our destination a few more emergency stops were made, and as we drove into the parking lot of our hotel the men were in direr straights due to the puzzled motive they had encountered, and they were bed ridden. An exploratory examination of their second sandwich discharged a fowl odor as well as green beef, and the culprits of their benefits were seized and discarded. The cost to the team was somewhat crippling in view of the fact that they could not render help with the testing program for some time during the unit's critical evaluation period. How often we hear the phrase; "If it sounds or seems too good to be true then more than likely it is."

The problem of life's development is that everyone is on his or her own, as all humans takes life's matters into their own hands, and feels unobligated to follow the wise admonishment of others. The word adult is adorned with the superior human view that we follow our best judgment. We often accept' our demise as a right to do it the wrong way, and the value of the word it, is germane to man's perception of infinity. God help us!

And so under these circumstances I was always inquisitive about the out come of the phrase: "follow your best judgment". When my comrades desire a bit of nightclub action, I was quite a reliable hand, since I did not drink. I did this necessary good not only for my team, but for any military comrade when it was compulsory. On one occasion I was in a group of candidates attending a Basic Noncommissioned Officer's course at Fort Carson, Colorado. We were free for the weekend, and my colleagues thought it would be entertaining to visit the clubs where the women showed more than their cleavages, so they signed me up for the trip to a life of sin without giving me notice given that they were under the influence. Consequently, I was convinced of the understanding that they would surely end up in jail if the law caught them in possession of the wheel; therefore, out of compassion I manned the drivers seat as they pledge to buy me all of the none alcoholic beverages necessary to quench my desire for the duration of their excursion. I courageously drove the drunks from strip club to strip club as I endure the persecution of many backseat drivers. I would park the van and then stroll in the place which smells like vagina only to observe the action of men putting dollar bills in dancers' draws. I find no pleasure in parting with my money so easily but these are the games adults' play, thus after having my fill I would go outside and just stand around in wait.

Virtual gigolo Sergeant Manning had a family and kids. Being set apart from her due to our military leadership course, he was at that moment let loose away from the carefully scrutinized eyes of his spouse, and he dabbled in the spirits and the festive ballets of naked women. He got shit-face drunk and could not control his composure and the girls continued their merry dance along with appeasing the high points of the audiences' expectation by relieving themselves of their clothes and emplacing plastic devices into their private parts. Suddenly the man's real brain (the brain in his penis) took control and as he inserted his hard earned greenbacks into her draws he hastily stuck his tongue into her vagina, since the gaping hole was uncovered and the string between it's right and left lips was designed to have a licentious effect, and it did. Everyone was startled, given that the name of the game was to fantasize the moment, without touching the subject or subjects in play. Well, as expected, that was against the rules, and they almost threw my comrades head over heels out of there. I was quite certain that that specific strip joint was a whore house; yes, I am 100% certain that that was a place where a man could get a quickie. So, you the reader ask how could I say such a thing. Well, I saw a man and a woman indulging in what seems to be a quickie. It was quite obvious. Anyway, we departed with a quickness before they call the law.

I openly and truly confess that I am fascinated by sparsely dress girls; however, I do not like them that mush that I would stick my fleshy tongue into a whole that I do not know anything about, due to my moral views and the reliability of modern pestilences to douse the light of ones life permanently. And by the way, I love my spouse and kids; therefore, I avoid all such troubles. But you have not heard the end of it yet, the fact of the matter is that, what people yearns for behind close doors is not always right for good relationships or their wellbeing. That same week Sergeant Manning got a bit of bad news that he did not cherished; but the circumstance was partly due to his own fault. His wife who was now by her lonesome at Fort Irwin, in the wide open spaces of the California desert was also experiencing a bit of her long yearning fancy. To be exact, it was a presumed glee of extramarital experimenting with Sergeant Manning's best friend. After entangling herself with the strange penis, the excitement lasted but for a moment, and two to three days later she developed a strong consciousness of cold feet as she fell into a posture of anxiety and depression, due to her consensual poking, and the shame of orally masturbating the strange male organ. Consequently, the engagement in extramarital rendezvous did not fill her longing desire as perceived within her fancy, and forthwith she called her loving husband begging for his forgiveness as the strange semen which dripped from her crotch flickers from her undergarment in the washroom. Hearing the bad news he lost all concentration and requested to be dropped from the roll. Before he departed to comfort his darling wife, he explained to us that he ask his friend to take care of his wife while he was away. I then wandered why I would ask my best man friend to take care of my spouse while I am away. To be true to the fact and life's realities, in his best judgment he probably would.

Some people's best judgment is the worst nightmare of others, and in this case it was. Never tell someone to follow their best judgment or when dealing with important matters always give them the judgment you would like them to follow, then you will be right in sink with your best judgment. For instance, an SUV (sport-utility vehicle) pulling a trailer sped pass my vehicle while I was traveling southbound on Interstate Highway 76 (I76) in the beautiful state of Colorado during the winter season. It was rather obvious to me that the vehicle was going in excess of 65 miles per hour (mph) since I was holding my own at about 60 mph on the icy road. Over the hill it went, as the driver who was following his best judgment drove pass my perceived horizon. Ten minutes later as I crested one of the many rolling hills which gives the highlands its beauty, I saw my prediction upside-down in the median and the occupants who had safely exit the disaster policing their belongings which were thrown from the trailer. I stop to assist the endangered fellow colleagues of the human species. They seemed to be in shock; however, it was all of their doing, since they were following their best judgment.

Within the previous milieu, I should have informed Sergeant Hypocrite Symons what my best judgment was on the idea of telling the wives everything we did, when we go to various towns to train National Guard soldiers. This was my first time on duty with him. Furthermore, out of respect as comrades, he could have informed us of his motives or his regularities on in-house matters. Anyway, let's get to the main tale at hand.

During our home away from home the team members invited me to a best choice setting to eat dinner. They assured me that it was a good restaurant and that I would like it. In my expectation to attend the unsurpassed of Granada's finest place of dining, my colleagues pulled into the parking lot of the Hooters den. My first impression as the vehicle came to rest in the parking area was "Oh shit, the wives, to be specific my wife will surely take this little blunder the wrong way if and when she finds out." To be fair, and forbearing a liberal minded scholar would say that going to the Hooters den to eat buffalo wings was quite Ok. However, to a speculative minded person the charge would be "why the hell are you going to Hooters den when you have never done so before?" The kicker to this reality would be the subtle question of: "What else are you doing when you go on these trips?" These are legitimate questions since I the author, a well entrenched GI (soldier) knew exactly what befalls many of my weak comrades on such night-outs away from home. Due to the fact that most GI's marriages are less than 50% solvent, when a comrade desires to do good, he must steer clear of all questionable activities or inform his spouse of such before others do. Mark my words, "A good relationship harbors no secrets." There are many men who runs' around God's great earth thinking that they can do what they want because they are Gods gift to women and their manhood gives them the license to be licentious. These are the same fools who usually cries foul, as well as they are all wroth and broken when they finds themselves on the opposite side of the divorcé trench.

I had never been on a mission with Hypocrite Symons, but it was too late now since the monkey had already jumped out of the cage, and this I did not know. We were successful in completing our mission. The troops that were found deficient in their skills were retrained and retested, and the team members were all safely back in the arms of their spouses in Hattiesburg, Mississippi. A week had pass and all was going well when my loving wife confronted me with a play by play story of our doings when I was in the community of Grenada, Mississippi. It was all true except for one diminutive detail which had no effect on the reality of the subject in point: my spouse.

"So, you went to the club. Did you have a good time?" She asks.

"What club?" I replied.

"The one you, Symons and the rest of you went to," she replied.

"We did not go to any nightclub," I said.

"Symons told Abigail everything, and he said that you guys went to a club."

"Symons?" I paused as I try to recall the events of our doings to memory, now being conscious that the next word I uttered could cause a needless up-roar. Many a GI's families suffered from similar evils which all turned out to be true. One thing leads to another; on the other hand, I had nothing to hide, so I am opt to tell her the truth. Nevertheless, it is quite difficult to reveal the truth to an idea or an accusation you know nothing about.

Silence covered our spaces. She smiled. We looked at each other.

My wife, "Speechless? I smell a rat."

"No, no rat! I am just wandering why Sergeant Symons had to go home and tell his wife that we went to Hooters?"

"The Hooters den? Looking for more attractive cleavages? "

"Yes, the Hooters den. Not so, your cleavage is just fine for me."

My wife have never bin into the Hooters restaurant, but the adds on the billboards defines the environment, and even if she did, she would not like the idea of me just going to a restaurant all by my lonesome to admire girls in skimpy short pants and T-shirts which flaunt the boobs. On the other hand, Hypocrite Symons left the door wide open by not explaining that we did not go to a night-club. And all my wife knew was that Abigail's husband was open about his doings and I was not. Thus, it was hard to convince the love of my heart that I did not go on a night-out in search of better boobs and whatever else goes with it. It was a stupid argument but so are many of life's realities.

Some skeptics may say that she is too controlling. I say that she is correct to be a cynic, in view of the facts that the military trend around her was quite disappointing. Nightclub gallivanting was not my lifestyle, and if I concocted a change of life's routine into a sudden novel glee of dances and girls, that could be a sign of trouble in the foreseeable future. A married man's kingdom is a home with his wife and kids. There is no future in a life of carousing without the wife and kids. There are lots of family fun in a life of marriage, and a glee of riotous party behavior with strange acquaintances of the opposite sex just does not fit into the family's puzzle. It was an argument within the manner of the dim-wits, and once you have been drawn into such a circle, it is very difficult to emerge victorious. Sometimes it is better to say nothing and keep a cool head, as your one hundred and thirty pound tiger pounces from room to room. In the end Abigail and my wife figured out the differences and I was off the hook. The real thing here is that men who act loud and boisterous outside of the home are relatively pussycats in their den. Their claim of being at the helm of their habitat is quite the opposite of what you think would be their best judgment, since they are prone to follow their best judgment and spill their guts without the thought of putting others at risk. Be sure that you are up on your game, as in giving your friends a hint of what is your best judgment. In that context you may be afforded the sanity of their best judgment; hence, you will be able to jump the gun successfully. It is not recommended that you become a learner in the midst of hostilities, if you care about your significant other.

Author: Allen M. D. Muckraker, ©

Sex At The Office

Antony Grayson is a young man of modest means and composure. He's not more than 27 years old or so and as a source of pride and youthful status he visits the gym on a regular basis. His job is quite the obvious: a soldier. On the other hand, due to the fact that we are in millennial times, we may identify him as a spoke in the wheel of the Americans world's policeman.

He loves his wife Meryl passionately, who's two years older, and is willing at a pounce to offer his life in exchange for her safety at any moment. To say the least, they are mortally tied at the waist, and are also linked by thoughts at the head. Telepathy would be an understatement of the intimacy betwixt them both. When observed by others, they appear to be inseparable.

Antony is presently on duty at a military unit's in-house academy's office not too far from what he and Meryl calls home. It is almost 4 O'clock PM and his wife made an unannounced visit to his work space. The classroom was deserted and the only sound in the building was that of a strong southwardly gust of wind that made a ghostly whistling hum as it seeps into the cracks of the wooden building. Such a taunting sound would put anyone in an empty building on edge, as the mind creates its own assertion of the current surroundings. The eeriness of a Halloween blitz gave air to a burst of life and contentment as Meryl walk into the classroom. She also affirmed an err of danger. As a result, before entering the uninhabited space she calls…

Allen?

He hears her voice, and abruptly stopped what he was doing and heads into the open space. She sees him as she stuck her head into the door-way. An altered spirit of the living engulfed the vacant classroom as he welcomed her with open arms and a kiss. After replenishing a famished need which had overcome its welcome, they meandered to the office where Allen was tinkering with the then top of the line software: Harvard graphics.

As they chattered away, the wolf in Allen was made present as the sense of nature overtook him. He now smells the shampoo in his wife's hair and the fresh fragrance of the soap on her person. He moved his chair close to hers and woe's her into a mood of submissiveness. Although she was nervous about the outcome, as she straddled his legs on the chair, and pulled her draws to one side, and let his hard shaft into her warm smooth embrace, ecstasy was contentment. The rush and perils of public mating was exhilarating, and the assimilation of such with the up and down jerking of the bodies had a profound affect on her arousal in such a way that she came in less than a minute. Subsequently, Allen was free to release his load to define the moment. Fifteen minutes later a cleaning-person opens the door and walk into the room.

Strange But True

During the later days of July 2010 two American soldiers were targeted for abduction by loyalist belonging to the Group of Madrasa Students (The Taliban) in Afghanistan as they were driving around in a theater of war in a civilian type armored automobile. One died in the ensuing firefight, and the enemy captured the other. As usual, the pundits talk and look down on the event and even reflects on the none affluent characters they supposed it takes to be an American fighting man. The military is a squeaky hygienic no fault organization. At least, this is how the tax payers see it, or imagine the force should be. Everything must be correct, due to the assumptions that soldiers are a little less than people in the public status realm, and just a tee wee bit below gods in the nationalistic realm. We are admired for killing people we have no business eliminating from God's great earth. When affluent people has an agenda they spends millions of dollars convincing the least educated of us that their cause is just and we like fools vote for them. They legitimately becomes presidents, senators, congress men and women, and even governors; and thereafter, discharges the nations assassins to accommodate their ideologies, most of which is to kill innocent people.

As soldiers returns home with scars from their nation's ideological business spree, they become jobless, homeless, a blight to the affluent and most often than not, young men and women become ill from a rash of what is called Post Dramatic Stress (This is when a fighting man or women becomes mentally impaired when they remember the killing they did, seeing others being killed or having the recollection of other uncommon destructive realities which occurs as men and women deploys the art of deliberately destroying other human beings).

Since the jury is out that all soldiers are most likely poor, illiterate and is not good to society but to kill people, then what does the same skeptics, pundits and affluent jingoists say about this? After military retirement I became a contract employee working as a manager responsible for the business of more than 600 foreign local company employees. The job paid well; however, I was only a spec in the daily affaires of the company. To be on the mark, I must say that the director of the company's business in theater had a smart for blending in. It became obvious on one occasion that someone thought that they saw a man of his likeness driving along the most dangerous highway (Highway 8 goes through the city of Baghdad to the renowned Baghdad International Airport) in Iraq. Upon closer scrutiny of the war time conundrum, it turned out that the said clairvoyant employee or employees were correct that the director of one of America's largest interpreter/translator contractor's which provided local and American Arabic interpreters to most of the units in theater was driving around the killing fields of Baghdad uninhibited in a private unarmored automobile all by his lonesome. Yes, the gifted one was my boss. Consequently, I must declare that soldiers are not special people, who are poor and retched, perfected in the art of killing people in the name of patriotism as a job. Anyone can be a fool and there are more fools in the civil sector than soldiers in the organization sanctioned to protect us. For whatever reasons, soldiers drive around battle fields in private automobile without military protection there is parallel rationale why civilians do the same.

Allen M. D. Muckraker

A Licentious Dan

And it was during the 1980s that Dan enjoyed a traveler's dream of being nomadic in Europe, as he took pleasure in the power of the dollar, and the frenzy of the European ladies in search of a liberated American GI. They were gold diggers in search of the American dream someone told them about. Dan acknowledges the American delusion as a myth, in view of the fact that paying a mortgage for 30 years is nothing else but a lawful form of highway robbery. Marriage is bliss, but it has its consequences which are many.

At the army barrack he was considered a saint who read his bible and prayed for the good of all of his comrades. On the outside of that lockbox his secrets grew far beyond the pale. Mannheim, Germany was his home base but he would travel to distant places by train, since it gave him an essence of freedom, due to it safety, alacrity and judicious schedule. Dan indulged himself in the culture of the host country, and night drifting was one of his favorites. He became as cunning as his counterparts, and the pleasure of capturing a beautiful girl became an art. Subduing a German damsel was common among his comrades; on the other hand, conquering a Turkish academic maiden without being hacked to death by her shielding relatives was more rewarding and an envious satisfaction.

It was an honest impromptus relationship as they spent many imaginative moments together, but it could not last, since she had to return to her studies in Frankfurt. They met near the city square in Mannheim on a summer night as she was in search of the train station on her way to Heidelberg. She was mesmerized by his kindness as he took her not only to the train station, but he accompanied her all the way to Heidelberg. As good as her companionship was relished for the summer; it was meaningful that the occurrence pass, due to the fact that he detected a pleasure of permanence in their accidental encounter. Dan was not the marrying kind, and a family of kids was not his idea of individual accomplishments. Summer departed and so did she.

It was now time to ride the train; a bit of miscellaneous lady snagging is in the works. Off he goes leaving the barrack behind, and many of his comrades who were mothballed in the building, incased in several bottles of booze. Dan was no normal enlisted soldier. He was quite adventurous, and his experience attested just that. He had an airplane license, and when he was bored and did not have enough time to travel he would fly his comrades around the base.

The European SOFA (Status Of Forces Agreement) drivers license was a coveted privilege due to the difficulty of the written exam given by a designated German test administer. There were about 150 signs and 100 questions on the test. If you miss more than a couple of each you were through, but the commander sign his admittance to the test and he aced it. This expansion of freedom gave him the ability to rent an automobile at his leisure; however, today he's taking the train to Frankfurt. A stop-off at the ATM kiosk not more than 500 feet away from his compound is a must, then he's off on the streetcar to the train station, and then on to Frankfurt by Simi-high-speed German train. He is a loose canon with a spending limit of less than five hundred dollars, but the exchange rate is superb. Dan is out fishing; furthermore, his intention is to run-a-muck at the clubs and have a good time. This is a simple GI solution to blow off steam after a difficult period of military training. He does this every 11 to 12 months or so, and the remainder of his time is spent as a miser. Dan's environment is imbedded in a cogent school of drug-attics, black marketers and unbendable adorers' of pornographic pleasures. His comrades smoke the weed openly in their refurbish Adolf Hitler's barracks. It was their little Amsterdam in our Mannheim encampment. Here, his military companions capitalized on their eligible chance of buying Uncle-Sam's nontax goods from the commissary/liquor store and sells it to desiring Germans. Of-course, it is against the rule, but who's watching? He stood his ground and indulges in none of such public sins except the one he could not avoid. The pornographic player was posted in the open-bays, and it exerted its will on him, in view of the fact that during leisure it was unavoidable. It played from morning till dust, and it corrupted him as it does many others to think with their peckers.

The train roared to a gentle motion and passengers can now see the landscape instead of a blur: fast-train. This means that Frankfurt main station is just minutes away. At last, the steel snake came to rest, and as the door gently opens, Dan did a quick visual recon of the area for damsels in distress.

Having no success, he trots lively along to destination nowhere. His carefree plan is the GI's norm: sample all the pubs on the strip, and hypnotize the weaklings of the opposite sex with his American charm, but at this moment in time on the first leg of his journey the reverse was true: he was not in command of his environment. Seconds after he entered his third club an expert of the trade lure him into her corner quickly. Her beauty was quite becoming, and he was not in control. By the way, money was not a factor, since in those days the exchange rate of the dollar to the Deutsche Mark (Germany's old currency) was three to one. Dan knew the game too well, but he decided to play along, since it was his time to splurge a-little. He bought a couple of drinks for her as she wished it, then she invited him to her den. This was a spacious room at the back of the club-house: he hopingly followed. There, they indulged in a bit of foreplay. After informing her that he was interested in the entire package, which she at this time was not. He wrote her off as a beggar and justified in himself that she was just another fun raiser for that club. But what the hell, a body is a body; they are all the same, and he now determined that he must try harder to subdue her for she was fair game. For good measure let's name Dan's new friend Delilah.

Suddenly, out of the blue, Delilah asked, where are you from?

Dan, "I'm from the Caribbean". Delilah, "How fortunate".

He explained the beauty of the clear blue seas, the white sand beaches and she loved his exaggeration of his homeland. And it was so that she dropped a troublesome snap on him in a gentle way. She meant him no harm. Delilah, "I'm from Israel". Dan eased backed into his seat and froze. He looked as though he had been spooked. You see, Dan was a religious man, and the last thing he wanted to do was to go a whoring with a daughter of God's chosen people. He pulled himself together, bid her farewell and went directly to the train station where he catch the first train out of Frankfurt. It was going to Mainz (a military town not far from Frankfurt). Dan's position is quite clear. Time and time again when Israel sinned against God, they got decimated. It is never good to be on the wrong side of the Almighty, and it is his concern that hanging-out with a promiscuous Israeli was a bad omen (A bad juju).

He is still in the party mood. Dan is dressed in black from head to toe. It is very dark outside, and there are no stars in the sky. Likewise, the club he chooses is a lively one not too far from the compound's gate, and the place is packed with party poopers. The lights are dim in such a way that it is difficult to see who is who. Dan steps inside and took-up residence in a corner over looking the dance floor. The crystal like turning globe in the midst of the lively commotion adds to the atmospheric frenzy that a dance hall should have. A young beauty caught his eye and she drifted over to his territory. Seated down, she introduces herself as an attractive one from Czechoslovakia. Instantly Dan cooked-up a plan. He is tired of buying drinks and not getting anything of substance in return. She draws close to him and as all of the others she requested a drink. No GI in their right mind actually thinks that these girls are truly drinking alcohol. This would be impossible, for surely they would be overwhelmed by such heavy doses of the named organic compound of the hydroxyl groups. There's more than one way to skin a cat and this was a cat that he was determined to skin. And the boldness of this plan was that he was going to achieve this scandalous act in a public place.

Muckraker's Folly

Ok, game on. He honored her request with her hearts desire. Thus, they had a merry chat. It was now time for him to make his move and he did. Sometimes a shocking intrusion into someone's private spaces results in quite an amenable reaction. Seated next to his new friend in the corner behind the table, Dan unzipped his zipper and prepared for battle. He did not know how she would receive the gesture, but if there is anything individuals in the civil sector must know, soldier's take giant leaps under gun-fire and also humongous daring's during licentious unfavorable circumstances. For instance, if you are facing a belligerent bully, the last thing that intimidator expects you to do is rise up and slap the hell out of him. Same principle, soldiers of other nations do not expect American fighting-men to mount a frontal charge under heavy machinegun fire. These girls were very nice bullies. They knew that the sexually depraved GI's were ripe for the taking, and they would run their flirting games until they run him out of money. In the dark, at the table they huddled nose to nose. Dan took her hand and genteelly places it on his crutch, and thus his stiff protruding organ. She melted. Silence. Dan broke the stillness that engulfed them both; knowing that he had won; a shrill of accomplishment beset him. He asked, "You like it?

Her reply was cuddled with nervousness, and the yes came with an agreement of shaking the ahead up and down. Dan now being empowered with such great success thought of having her do the unthinkable right there in a dark corner, in full display of the public's view. Given that she was conquered and within the riddle that she did not let go of the hard sensation in her left hand, as well as everyone else was getting busy dancing in the dark, he massaged her long blond hair for a moment, and with a quick action he brought her head to the point of no return. Thus, she followed through, and did the unthinkable to his and her astonishment. Unfortunately, her head was below the table a bit too long, and someone in her group noticed, thus their entanglement came to an abrupt halt. Dan tidied-up himself, rush out of the building to the station, and catch the midnight train to Mannheim. Author: Allen M. D. Muckraker ©

Green Card Lost In Syria

It was in Zakho that Allen the American met Marsha and her brother Mark. There, they labored as hands of the post units' chef in the kitchen in Zakho. The young damsel heard that Allen was looking for linguist and she made it her business to do whatever it took to come see him. The one to two hundred dollars a month she and her brother garnered from the slave like labor of washing and cleaning up after the foreigners' in her country projects a similarity of malnutrition in her skinny hands and legs. There was also another brother, whom by tradition had become the head of the family. Unfortunately, his body was in a cast as he recovered from an accident that broke a rib or a shoulder (not sure which one it was) on his previous job. Her mother, who resides with them is encumbered by tradition and does not work. Therefore, Marsha and Mark provides for their family. The twist to these young peoples overwhelming predicament was that they had grown up in America. The hollowed reflection in their countenance enlightens true hopelessness due to their family's choice to repatriate their mortally ailing father, so that he may expire in Zakho, Iraq. Their mother, a traditional woman, took the kids out of school just before graduation to perform the journey of faith. Allen was not too sure who were or if any were citizens but Marsha and Mark, about nineteen to twenty years old had American green cards in their pockets.

When they were all done with their fathers' ceremonial wishes, they were now on a tight budget. Yearning for the good life in America, they instantly begin their journey through the maze of Syria for a return to the real land of flowing milk and honey. What occurred next would seal their faith as fools. Although Allen feels for the Kids, he realizes that this is what happens to clueless people if they do not have first class knowledge about the vagabonds in the Middle East. On the other hand, how come we as elders admonish the little ones not to talk to strangers, and knowing the dangers we fail to follow our own advice, and thus falls head long into the soup.

To school those of you who doe not know about the flexibility of the American green-card, here is the truth as per traveling with the American resident card. If you have a valid passport from your country and your American green card, no visa is needed to enter the United States of America. The bearers of the American resident card just have to keep those documents current and they may come and go as they please.

Muckraker's Folly

For some unknown reason the mother of the kids gave a Syrian thug their passports along with some money to get through Syria, and the documents were never seen again. They ran out of money with airplane tickets in hand, as they tried to retrieve the traveling documents. Thereafter, they somehow made their way back to Iraq.

The dilemma is real, they were now stuck, and the kids would not be able to graduate. Furthermore, all of Marsha's freedom as an American female teenager was now curtailed as she and her mother commands the veil. The head scarf is the rule and her brothers now say what she can and can not do. As Allen listened to their story, and identifying the documents in their hands, he gave them the best advice he could, and complemented that by hiring them both as interpreters.

They were not the only ones who fell into that category, because Allen also met another Middle Eastern American (not too sure if he was citizen or resident) who sent in his résumé, and was summoned to report for one of those $130,000.00 contract jobs in Iraq. Not to say the least, his interview was in the good old USA, and you guess it, he did not have the money for the plane ticket to return to the land of plenty. The government does not allow the companies to hire for such critical positions from outside of the United States, since there is more to it than just filling out an application. Many have their keys to the gates to the land of plenty; however, they are living in dire straights due to their own doings or default curse.

In light of pass sleazy revelations of the Syrians, they may not be able to pass-up a good deal. Thinking as a Syrian vagabond, what do you think that the Taliban is trying to do with those American documents right now?

Patrol In A Korean Heaven

1985 was a good year for my dear uncle: Uncle Sam that is. During that year I had a well planned-out civilian future, but my uncle tricked me into biting a soft carrot, and since I ate the whole thing, I was in like flint. A twenty thousand dollar check was big money back then, and due to my gourmand like demeanor, I was blinded by the awesome amount of greenbacks he offered me to stay on with the troops. As I made peace with my dear uncle, I declared that he was always up to no good but so was I, and it seemed as though we were good for each other. In all realities and memories, Germany was a blast. In those days, unknown to our commander, during nightfall in the midst of the well orchestrated field exercises, the local Germans brought the booze, and other nice things to the bushes (the bivouac). We policed the trash and all other evidences by daybreak, and were always well mannered in the morning at the continuation of training hostilities. Off to South Korea I go on a new assignment, and thus, I am thrust into an effort to assist in quelling old ill wills and political evils of the pass and I in my heart of hearts am expecting no less than the same scandalous behavior in the South Korean sphere as that which effortlessly entices the minds of the American GIs in the Bavarian lands.

The new millennial soldier's are quite petite in their imagination; they talk too much and will never experience the equivalent. When I got to Camp Casey nearing the local town of Tongduch'ŏn it was spring and the friendly people of South Korea were wallowing in the luscious green fields. To initiate our coming, the army took the new arrivals to the well know 1953 armistice site of Panmunjom where we could see the north up-close and their willingness to continue the laborious efforts to be separatist. On that same day a couple of school buses filled with kids were also visiting the war museum at the site and while the other American soldiers thumped their noses at the little ones that did not look like them, I joined their company and we had a blast as we exchanged friendly gestures and poses for pictures with each other. And although I would be keeping an open eye on the mischievous north and their doings, I had determined that this tour of duty was going to be a good one.

In those days, the army still had a few faithful bigots belonging to the Ku Klux Klan in its ranks, and I even ran into a bit of opinionated jaunt with some of the sleazes; but by and large, the greater percent of the unit was free minded and we got along great. Natures greatest malevolence which befallen me in the Korean Heaven was the inflammation of the lungs. The educated ones call this pneumonia, and as the lesser of us can see, they spelt it in such a way to confuse us. It was a trial for life, and I won. Furthermore, the vigorous struggle resulted in a cash of lost weight and a bit of abated training which was all devised by my dear uncle. Without a doubt, I made haste to be ready for our next field exercise, and I was in like flint. The M60A1 tank was our best technology yet, and we used it to scare the bastards on the other side of the dividing lines. We practice crossing through the Imjin Gang and the engineering of the path was as the dividing of the Nile River, and it was a sight to see our iron horses rolled in and out of the waters. As we held ground, we did a bit of patrolling and the foot march afforded us an opportunity to seize the day.

Our commander watches with delight as he gazed at his none-infantry tank crew men made good of the hour on a march in simulation to save a near by town. Being content with our performance, he scurried off to inspect the other platoons. At last we were alone and now not more than a stone throw away from the entrance to unknown expectations. Our orders; do not go into town. But in our zeal to obey our captain and turn around before breaching the village, a festive bunch in a plot before the gate seems to be beckoning for our presence. I quickly informed the platoon sergeant of my awareness, but he seems to be not interested. We foot the march for about three hundred feet more, and were given the signal to halt. Giving it no credence, we got into our positions and covered our sectors of fire with vicious realization. Up comes another signal to backtrack and in doing so, the point-man led us unswervingly into the heart of the festivities. Nothing could have been better. It was a day to remember as we dabbled in the likeness of Soju and the delicacy of bulgogi and rice wine. Our Korean host was gracious, and he invited us to talk to the bride and groom. We were happy and content to be disposed ambassadors for our country as we stumbled by way of the long route back to camp. We were men of glee; empathically the likes of our dear uncle: Uncle Sam.

Author: Allen M. D. Muckraker, ©

Hay Boy! Colonel Wants Your House

Jefferson James was a friend of mind, and a well mannered as well as a smart member of our small detachment of observer controllers in Hattiesburg, Mississippi. Our ultimate mission was to train the Mississippi National Guard, and bring them up to the military standards of a federal fighting force. To be blunt, we were not welcome when we first arrived, and the guard's men received us with contempt of the notion that were mandated by the army to alter the culture of their southern military tradition. In their best judgment, the Mississippi National Guard utilized their weekend training sessions as a means of wanton beer excursion for many years, and it resonated in their performance when they came to Fort Irwin, California for unit's certification evaluation training.

In the desert at Fort Irwin, California was where I first experienced the tricks of the Mississippi militia. At this time, and during this critical moment of hostilities, their display of the spirit and bravery of an American element of war was lest than gallantry in their train up to be deployed to Gulf War One. The investigation of the entire unit was held in the class room wherein I taught new arrivals to the desert training post our mission, culture and the way we fight. Sad to acknowledge the obvious, but their state of readiness at a time when the country was counting on them was negative 10 below the Grenadian defense junta of the 1980s. To be blunt, if they were the tip of our spear, we would have had our ass handed to us by men with sticks and stones. The revelations discovered during the investigation were despicable, (I am not at liberty to say what was revealed) and their leadership core was removed in disgrace. This was my first encounter with the bastard bunch. So, for good military reasons, the federal government brought in the military game changers, and I was one of the first that was sanctioned to accomplish the task during the latter part of 1990. To say the least, some of the guards' men were rather scoundrels, as well as others were good at their military duties. However, the negatives were more than the positives and at one of the unit's evaluation I was offered money to give a passing grade. I courteously decline the offer to be corrupted, and took more time and showed more respect for the soldier, as I taught him the correct way to perform his primary military duty. He later departed my station a happy camper.

Even though there are minuscule remnants of bigotry in the hearts of the old farts in the town of Hattiesburg, Mississippi, the young inhabitants have overshadowed the naïve, backward thinking of their up bringing, and things are more hunky-dory now. The Ku Klux Klan still lives in the hearts and soul of the aged Mississippians. As a matter of fact, I have identified their yearning to be in the old Circle of the villains, given that during a brigade unit's forum, many old-farts in the State's National Guard questioned military legal representatives about the legality of being a member of the debunk terrorist

Muckraker's Folly

Confederate Circle which intimidated Americans at will. The zany bunch could not understand why the military outlawed such a contemptible organization since it was in their character to be that way. They were not pleased with the answers received. Now, to make things more the merrier, and a challenge to the GI's (the soldier's) stamina to resist Delilah, Southern Mississippi State University is centered directly in the heart of the civic seen, and by far, many of the young attendees do not wear any draws. In view of the fact that there were no military housing at that time all regulars resided within the civil community. A few of my comrades got caught in the scuffle with the vicious girls who were looking for husbands, and their marriages folded quickly, since the power of the young damsels were hypnotizing. I've even learned a few things in that southern heaven as I moonlighted a job or two in my spear time, of which I will only reveal a few details.

The first southern expressive muddle is the phase Chinese overtime. What the hell is that, I proclaim in my obligatory assimilated southern ignorance. In due time, I was to be enlightened, and the enlightenment came in the form of an assistant manager. As many would call them; the manager's gofers.

However, there can only be one manager and someone has to be a gofer. The situation is similar to the governor and lieutenant governor's state of affairs, where the lieutenant governor hopes for the quick demise of the governor, so that he can become the governor. Working at this little store was quite an excitement sometimes, the police send minors into the store to check to see if the cashiers would sell the snotty nose little people forbidden goods such as cigarettes, and alcohol beverages. At other times it was a thief with a pack of chicken under his or her garments. Then we had the courageous brights, one of which includes none other than the foxy sixteen year old daughter of the store chain owner. She thought that she would get a pass on buying beer since her father owns the store. The trick did not workout in her favor; and last but not least, we had the glee bunch: the party poopers. After we close the doors to the store at nights, sometimes a number of my fellow workers would remain inside, and the jovial mix of beer and intercourse was the highlight of the next day itinerary.

Certain occurrences could only happen in the culture of country ethics, and in a place where the black man rant and rave in a fierce fight for recognition, the brown vagina is a prized possession in the south. If there ever was to be a sign that says no Negros allowed. You should qualify that statement to mean brown girls are very welcome here, especially those that are half breed. Early one night I was free and I went down to the job placement office to fine work. That Friday evening I was sent to work at the USA TODAY printing press to earn my due. A fine young thing was included in the accompanying group of day earners. The foxy chocolate thing could turn heads in her wake, and if you were on the largest ship in the world in still waters, you would do nothing less than feel the current passing as you drew near her presence. Everything went well until missy realized that she was the epicenter in the production room. She stop working and callously spent most of her time talking to those who drool at her presence and complexion as they do less work. All of this feminine whoa about her must have been astounding, due to the fact that she was just another half-breed in her native neighborhood. Yes, she had the Mississippi twang complexion. On my tour of duty in that southern state, many a times I'd ran into albino like colored folks who's Negro like hair was the only resemblance of them being a black person. Consequently, I must declare that the Mississippi masters were plague with an obsession of dipping more than their fingers in the pudding. To make matters worse, and to her delight, not only that some of the black guys found her favorable, but the energized white guys engendered a mysterious fondness that she was sexually appetizing: per se. Our supervisor who was black noticed that she was not up to her bargain. At least in his mind, she was there to put newspapers which fell out of the assembly line back together. She held no sway with him. He gave her two stern warnings and being too tolerant at last he threatened to send her home if she did not improve. She was quite displeased as she reported him to the manager of the night, and forthwith after her return, to everyone's surprise the white manager send the black supervisor home for the night instead. Therefore as shocking as it was to understand the phrase "Chinese overtime" after a demonstration of southern hospitality such as the one I just recently described became a normality, and I expected nothing better for the remainder of my military duty as I live with the Mississippians.

Oh before I forget, here is the meaning to the puzzle of the phrase "Chinese overtime." I notice that Jim the assistant manager was working on the dayshift and he remained on the nightshift on the same day also. Taking notice of this unusual event, I had a chat with him about the subject.

"Hi Jim" I said.

He replied in an un-joyous manner, and I was taken back because of his unhappy response. Hmm, I said, not too happy ah?

He replied, "No."

I interjected just as he was about to say something. You should be happy, goodness man you are on overtime, and that was when he let the displeasure of his soul out into the air and proclaimed his dissatisfaction with the Mississippians ancient labor system. I have rummage around a little bit, and failed to find anyone who would acknowledge that the system exist. He doled out his displeasure and it goes like this.

"You see, normally when someone works overtime they get time and a half."

I shook my head in agreeing with him. He continued

"But in Chinese overtime after you work your due, you get half time."

I told him that I did not understand, and that he should break it down so that someone such as I who was ignorant in southern ethics could appreciate this new-fangled enlightenment.

Hence, he did. His reply was off the charts.

Jim, "I get paid $14 an hour now. If I work over time I should get $14 plus $7 more for each hour I work. I shook my head in agreement as I responded "aha, aha, aha."

I thought that things were bad, in the old enclave state of narrow-mindedness but I did not expect it to be this bad, and in these modern times poor white people also get the boot.

Jim, "Now! At this moment I make $7 per hour."

My response was futile, since I knew that this store chain even have a big turboprop aircraft, and my flight instructor was the corporate pilot who flew the modern marvel to whatever destination pleases the owner. Therefore, the owner of the chain of stores had the cash to pay, but as all gluttonous rich people he raped the poor to suite his fancy.

"Are you serious" I said.

He answered "Yep."

"Is this legal?" I shouted.

He staid silent: no response.

I continue, "I don't think that it is legal, and I bet you that the government doesn't think so either."

We both went silent.

This was the environment that Colonel Done thrust himself into. His twin brother was a general, and he the Colonel got so far away from military reality that he forgot the official code of ethics with bearing emphasis on selfless service. Furthermore, he failed to grasp the fact that he was still in the U.S. army, and unbecoming an officer could be as slight an evil as removing a subordinate and his family from his place of residence in order to please his civilian friend was beyond the vale of a commission officer in the most powerful military in the world. He is a perfect example of the disgraced Afghanistan U.S. General named Stanley McCrystal who thought that his status of being a four star general would save him from demise as he disrespected the commander in Chief of the U.S. military.

So one of Colonel Done's colleague in his civilian neighborhood (elite gated housing association) organization wanted the house that Colonel Done's soldier: Jefferson James resides in. The alleged home buyer informed Sergeant Jefferson James that he wants the house he was renting, and that he was going to have to move because Colonel Done was going to take care of the details. Sergeant James hearing that his Colonel was in on the deal, decided to have a talk with his superior in lieu of the fact that if this is true, it would be illegal according to military codes of ethics for his superior to indulge in such unwholesome behavior. During the babbling scuffle Colonel Done and Sergeant James was not seeing eye to eye, and Colonel Done a superior commissioned officer assure the sergeant that he can take his leased property away from him if he chooses and there was nothing he could do about it. Sergeant James being wiser than the egotistical Colonel who was now acting as a civilian, turned to the military for help by way of the whistleblowers phone line; consequently as a result, Colonel Done was done with the army. Case solved. Monkey-ing around with hooligans usually causes nothing other than trouble, and Colonel Done learnt his lesson the hard way. No one is above the law, at least that is the catch phrase, and when government officials blunders and cause thousands of human casualties they should pay the price just as commoners do. It would be very satisfying to see our first president, vice president, secretary of state, congressman or woman, white house chief of staff, governor and lieutenant governor all in the lockup for mismanagement of soldier's lives and the nations cash cow: the peoples taxes. Then and only then, elected and appointed leaders would think twice before they cause the mass slaughtering of others (None of their own) for the reason that they acted on erroneous or false information.

Author: Allen M. D. Muckraker, Copy rights reserve ©

I hope that you enjoyed your read. Thanks for visiting Muckraker's heaven.

Muckraker's Folly

Author: Allen M. D. Muckraker

www.ingramcontent.com/pod-product-compliance
Lightning Source LLC
Chambersburg PA
CBHW070007300526
45794CB00001B/227